TASTE OF MALTA

A Collection of Maltese and Traditional Recipes

ANTON B. DOUGALL

BDL Publishing
© Book Distributors Limited
www.bdlbooks.com

Copyright of recipes © Anton B. Dougall
Typesetting and design by © Book Distributors Limited

First published 2014
Reprinted 2015, 2018, 2019

Taste of Malta
A Collection of Maltese and Traditional Recipes

Photography by © Oliver Gatt - www.olivergatt.com
pg 27 - Ken Scicluna

ISBN Paperback: 978-99957-46-28-5
Hardback: 978-99957-46-32-2

Printed by Print It, Raħal Ġdid

dedicated to my mother
Julia,
a true homemaker

CONTENTS

AROMATIC HERBS & SPICES

Dr Antoine Vella D.Sc.Agr. (Milan), Ph.D.

Antoine Vella is a lecturer at the Institute of Earth Systems (Rural Sciences and Food Systems Division) of the University of Malta. He holds a degree in Agricultural Sciences from the University of Milan and a Ph.D. from the University of Malta.

AROMATIC HERBS & SPICES

Nowadays, aromatic herbs and spices are an essential ingredient of many recipes from all over the world, but it is almost certain that they were first used for medicinal purposes and only later came to be appreciated as flavourings. Nobody knows how their effects on health were discovered, but we do know that the Sumerians used thyme and laurel some 5,000 years ago. The ancient Egyptians, Greeks and Romans also used herbs, not just as food and medicine, but also as cosmetics.

It is interesting to note why nature has given some plants the characteristic chemical composition that renders them so appetising to humans. Ironically, the pungent substances which distinguish them are produced as a protection against browsing herbivores. Essential oils and other substances render the leaves bitter and unpalatable and only the most desperate, starving animal would eat them! For some reason, however, humans enjoy the taste; said plants, though, have to be used in very small concentrations as the flavour can otherwise become overpowering and unpleasant.

Different types of herbs can be found more or less everywhere, but normally the ones with the strongest flavours are those growing in poor, stony soils and scrubby areas. Again, there is a biological explanation for this: the vegetation of rich, fertile soils is made up of a large number of plant species; hence, there is a wide

selection for herbivores to choose from. This means that the herbs need only a small quantity of the aromatic ingredient to discourage the animal from eating them. At the first nibble, the bitter taste compels the animal to move on to a different plant, as long as there are other species available.

The choice is much more limited in poor areas so much that browsing animals have to survive on whatever vegetation they can find. In this environment, plants need to have a higher concentration of the aromatic ingredient in order to persuade the animal to desist from eating their leaves. This explains why two of the best habitats for herb production are the upper slopes of mountains such as the Alps where the soil is thin and the climate quite harsh and the Mediterranean garigue which is basically a surface of dry, windswept rock with occasional pockets of poor soil. This happens to be the most typical natural habitat in small, rocky islands such as Malta, Lampedusa and the like, and explains why herbs from such places are the most sought after.

There is yet another reason why Maltese herbs are of better quality than those produced elsewhere. Throughout summer, the long days of bright, uninterrupted sunlight stimulate the plant, giving it energy and forcing its metabolism to work overtime. In theory the plant should grow and flourish but, because water is so scarce, the leaves and branches cannot develop properly and the plant remains stunted. What it does, instead, is to use solar energy to manufacture higher quantities of the aromatic substances

Mediterranean garigue

so that, by the end of summer, plants growing in garigue areas are extremely rich and have the strongest flavour. This is why herbs grown in pots and watered regularly cannot match their wild cousins as regards quality and flavour.

Therefore, it is only to be expected that while herbs are used everywhere, it is mainly in the areas bordering the Mediterranean that they acquire a primary role in the traditional cuisine. Since herbs have always been so important in everyday life, people who have no knowledge at all of botany are usually able to recognise and identify the different species growing locally. In every language, moreover, each herb has its own particular name usually derived from its medicinal use or, in the case of introduced species, from the name by which the plant was known in its country of origin. Thus, the Greek *minthe* became *menta* in Latin and then mint and *menthe*

Mint

in English and French respectively. The vernacular names are a clue to the history of that plant. Thus, the fact that mint has similar names in so many languages is a probable sign that originally it had a narrower range than at present and that it was carried by travellers and merchants from the Mediterranean to the rest of Europe.

On occasion, the origin of the name may even have been forgotten and the local population would then try to guess what the word means. This can give rise to some curious legends and folklore such as in the case of sage. In English, 'sage' means 'a wise man' and this herb became therefore associated with wisdom and was thought to improve one's memory. This belief was so widely held that a certain John Gerard, one of the most

renowned English Renaissance herbalists, wrote that "Sage is singularly good for the head and brain, it quickeneth the senses and memory, strengtheneth the sinews, restoreth health to those that have the palsy, and taketh away shakey trembling of the members" (Herbals or General History of Plants, 1597). Amazingly, all this 'ancient knowledge' was based on a misunderstanding. The word 'sage' in the sense of 'wise' is derived from the Latin *sapidus* from the verb *sapere* meaning 'to know'. The name of the plant, on the other hand, comes from the Latin *salvia* from the verb *salvare* meaning 'to save' and refers to the medicinal properties of the herb which were already well known to the Romans. Unfortunately, no matter how much sage one eats, one will never become sage!

Sage

Another herb whose name has repeatedly acquired a different meaning in time is rosemary. Today, many still think that the English name means 'Rose of Mary' in reference to Our Lady. In reality it is derived from Latin and its Roman name was thought to be composed of *ros* (dew) + *marinus* (marine); hence, rosemary was

supposed to be called in this way because it grew near the sea. It is now believed that the name is even older and comes from the Greek *rops* (bush) + *myrinos* (aromatic).

Rosemary

Incidentally, Maltese names of herbs are either of semitic origin as in the case of *naghniegh*, *klin*, *saghtar* and *habaq*, or derived from Italian as in the case of *rignu* or *salvja*. It is thought that the former, which are much more numerous, indicate plants which existed and were used during the Arab period (10th century) while the latter refer to plants probably introduced later. Although Malta is such a small island, it has a disproportionately high number of wild aromatic herbs – around 400 species. This has led some botanists to speculate that they are not all indigenous, but were introduced in Malta by Arab apothecaries.

The skilful use of herbs in the kitchen doesn't, obviously, require us to know either the biology or the history and culture surrounding the plants themselves, but it is always interesting to have some background knowledge about the ingredients that we use. It is wonderful to realise that when we carry out the simple gesture of putting one or two bay leaves in a stew, we are repeating the very same act that countless generations have been doing for the past 5,000 years. Life changes and so many civilisations have come and gone during these fifty centuries, yet the humble act of adding a natural flavouring to our food is literally timeless!

TYPICAL MALTESE FOOD PRODUCTS

AND THEIR ORIGIN

Eman Vella B.A.(Hons), P.G.C.E, MSc S.E.R.M.

Eman Vella graduated in 2003 from the University of Malta. In 2010, he graduated in a Master of Science in Sustainable Environmental Resources Management from the University of Malta and Master of Science of Integrated Science and Technology from James Madison University, U.S.A. He is currently employed as project manager at the Ministry for Sustainable Development, the Environment and Climate Change.

BEES AND HONEY

Since ancient times, the Maltese Islands have been known for their special blended honey. In fact, even though the origin of the name 'Malta' is uncertain, it is believed that it derives from the Greek word *meli* meaning 'honey'. Possibly this is due to Malta's unique production of honey. The best type of honey comes from the garigue landscapes in the North of Malta. The village of Mellieħa in particular is an important apicultural location principally for the gathering of wild thyme honey. Apart from the unique spicy taste, Maltese honey has been found to be useful for its healing properties, especially in the case of colds and cough. It is also used in desserts.

Honey is the produce of bees which live in colonies and work restlessly at all times of the day. The Maltese bee, scientifically known as *Apis mellifera ruttneri*, is completely black in colour and is most suitable for the Maltese climate. The species *Apis mellifera linguistica* is also a common bee in Malta and is recognised from its yellow circles.

Bee keeping in the Maltese Islands has a very long history as can be proven by the ancient bee apiary found in Xemxija. Nowadays, there are around 150 bee keepers in Malta and Gozo. Most bee

Pollen is highly important for the bees' nutrition and for their young. Bees collect nectar from flowers and agricultural products in season and produce honey from flower nectar. In spring time, bees collect nectar from various flowers and fruit trees. In summer, bees work on nectar from Mediterranean Thyme; in autumn, they feed on flowers of Carob and Eucalyptus trees. Once at the colony, this nectar is spread out in the various cells so as to remove the excess water which normally amounts to 80%. The bees add enzymes to further increase the honey's nutritive value. The cells are then sealed for conservation until the bee keeper collects the honey.

keepers have one or two colonies and keep bees as a hobby. Nevertheless, there are professional bee keepers who keep over 50 bee colonies for the production of honey and wax. Moreover, bees are important plant pollinators; some farmers in fact keep bee colonies to facilitate fruit pollination.

Typical honey product: *Qagħaq tal-għasel*

Qagħaq tal-għasel or honey-rings are a traditional sweet consumed during the Christmas season. Although their name indicates that they are made from honey, their actual filling is treacle (black honey). The pastry ring is filled with *qastanija*, which is the mixture made from treacle and other ingredients. Today, honey-rings are found all year round and can easily be bought from supermarkets and confectionery shops. Further details regarding this traditional sweet will be provided with its respective recipe given in the sweet section of this book.

WHEAT, BREAD AND WATER BISCUITS

Wheat is planted in autumn and early winter since the plant must be kept moist naturally through the soil as generally the farmer doesn't water this plant. Its only source of water is rain water; in fact, following a dry winter, there is a small amount of wheat to harvest. During the month of May, the wheat dries up and is

ready to be collected. Before the use of machinery, wheat was cut using a sickle. This tool has a wooden handle on one side and a flat, iron, half moon shaped blade on the other. Wheat collection, besides being time consuming, entailed very hard work when compared to today's mechanised cutting and collection methods.

During the months of June and July, farmers used to pick out a windy place in their fields where to hold threshing and winnowing in a process known as the *qiegħa*. The threshing floor used for the *qiegħa* had to be circular and the soil well trampled and dry. The dried wheat was placed on the ground and the farmer placed himself at the centre of this area. Animals such as horses and donkeys were tied together next to each other and the farmer directed them in a circular motion around the threshing floor through his central position. As they walked around, the animals stepped on the wheat and separated the grains from the stalks. The other members of the family would shovel all the wheat around so that the animals would thresh all of it.

Once all the wheat was stepped on, farmers waited for the right wind so as to blow away the hay and they were left with the most precious part of the wheat. This was then collected and passed through a number of sifters so as to clean it from dust and any other unwanted material. It was then ready to be taken to a mill and turned into flour or stored in sacks in the farmhouse. The straw was collected and stored to be used as animal bedding as well as fodder.

The main ingredient for bread is flour, which is blended together with salt, water and a raising agent. Traditionally, bread baking was a thoroughly handmade process. Bread was baked in stone ovens powered by burning wood. Summer heat helps the dough raising process and thus more salt is needed. In winter, the cold air slows down the raising process so the baker has to add more raising agent and lessen used salt. The dough is left to rise and then it is cut into pieces according to weight and shaped into bread. It is then placed into the oven. One particular tool worth mentioning is the wooden spade with a long handle able to reach all areas of the oven.

The Maltese bread maker prepares a number of products including the *ħobża tal-Malti* (Maltese, crusty, sourdough bread), which is found in two different sizes: the *ħobża tas-salib* and *ħobża tas-sikkina*. The former would have a cross sign on the top to be recognized as the last batch of bread placed in the oven and therefore the first ones to come out. The latter is the same kind of bread, but with a knife-cut on its top side. Maltese bakers also produce the *ftira*, a flat round bread, also found in two different sizes and baked on trays. The *bezzun* is a long, slim-shaped bread while the *panina* is round and small. A type of bread called

tal-kexxun is baked in a rectangular oven dish. One must point out that the baker's job is mostly done during the night so that the bread is ready to be freshly bought first thing in the morning.

Typical wheat product: *Galletti*

Another Maltese product made from wheat flour is the *galletti* or round water biscuits. These light, crispy biscuits are served along with dips as a starter or a snack and as accompaniment to cheeses at the start or end of a meal. *Galletti* are included in practically all Maltese platters and are also eaten as a quick snack.

MILK PRODUCTS

The production of milk is one of the oldest industries in the Maltese Islands. Traditionally, milk was bought on a daily basis directly from the farmer. Some goat and sheepherders also used to visit towns and villages with their sheep and goats that were milked directly into the customers' containers. However, in the 1930's, people who drank this unpasteurised milk started contracting undulant fever; thus, boiling milk before drinking was highly encouraged. Subsequently, a milk processing factory was built in Ħamrun and a milk collection centre opened in Qormi.

The small size of the Maltese islands allows milk to reach consumers within a very short span of time, usually less than

Malta

24 hours since it is milked. Other products derived from milk include yogurts, fresh cream, ricotta, mozzarella, white cheeslets and peppered cheeslets. Milk producing animals include cows, sheep and goats. Cows found in Malta are mostly from the Holstein-Friesian breed that is renowned for its high quality milk production at about 20 litres of milk per day. There are about 140 cow farms in Malta with a herd of 8,000 milking cows, producing over 42,000 tonnes of fresh milk.

Sheep milk is renowned for the production of *ġbejniet*, a cheeslet that can be eaten fresh or dry. Dried *ġbejniet* can be also found in a peppered version. Goats are reared for the production of cheese as well as for their milk. In the olden days, goats' milk was preferred; nowadays, this has been replaced with cows' milk.

Typical milk product: *Ġbejniet*

Ġbejniet (plural of *ġbejna*) are a favourite ingredient in *ħobż biż-żejt*, which is typically spread either with *kunserva* or fresh tomatoes and drizzled with olive oil. Fresh, white and peppered sheep *ġbejniet* are either found in most supermarkets packed in plastic containers or bought directly from producers. *Ġbejniet* are used in *soppa tal-armla*, a traditional vegetable soup, as well as a filling for ravioli and *qassatat* pies. Traditionally, *ġbejniet* are produced from sheep milk or a blend of sheep and goat milk.

Typical milk product: *Irkotta*

Irkotta is a traditional soft cheese made from warm sheep and goat milk that is cooked in an exact amount of boiling sea water. The cooking process takes about forty minutes, during which the milk is stirred continuously until it coagulates. The milk is then poured onto a sieve to separate the thickened milk from the *xorrox* (remaining liquid). Thickened milk left on the sieve is collected into small containers and left to cool to be served as *irkotta*. It is important to note that the Italian *ricotta* is different from Maltese *irkotta* as the former is made from a by-product of cheese and not from fresh milk.

OLIVES AND OLIVE OIL

The location of the Maltese Islands in the central part of the Mediterranean Sea makes them ideal for the production of olives and olive oil. This industry was important for the development of Malta along the centuries as can be witnessed by remains of olive crushing stones dating back to Punic and Roman eras. Nevertheless, this industry was disrupted in the middle ages when most olive trees were uprooted to make way for the cultivation of cotton. It is only lately that the olive oil industry is significantly increasing with olive trees being planted around the archipelago.

There are different varieties of olive trees grown in Malta. Some are ideal for the production of olive oil and others for the olive fruit. The most common olive tree varieties used for the production of olive oil are the *Frantoio, Leccino, Bianca Lille* and *Coratina*. Most common olive tree varieties used for table olives are the *Uovo di Piccione* and *Bella di Spagna*. There are also varieties that are grown both for olive oil production and for table olives such as *Carolea, Picholine* and *Nocellara Messinese*. Apart from these international olive tree varieties, there are also local cultivars, such as *Tal-Bidni,* that are lately being replanted in the quest to re-establish a local olive oil industry.

Olive oil is obtained by pressing olives in order to separate the liquid from the solid

content, which is then filtered and later preserved in specific temperatures and conditions. The traditional olive harvesting season is October when the olives start to turn black. They are then pressed soon after the harvest to avoid fermentation and low quality oil. Hand-picked olives produce superior olive oil since the fruit is not damaged. Olive oil is ideally preserved in sealed glass or stainless steel containers in a cool, dark place to avoid light and air intrusion that reduce oil quality.

Typical olive product: Olives in brine

A widespread rural traditional in the Maltese Islands is to have a stock of olives preserved in brine. Large olives are collected in October, washed and soaked in fresh water for a week. Then, they are placed in a container full of water and diluted sea salt, mixed with bay leaves and occasional herbs such as fennel or chilli. Olives are left to mature in brine for around four months, after which they are used in a number of local dishes.

MEAT AND ANIMAL PRODUCTS – RABBITS, PIGS, LAMB, BEEF, CHICKENS AND EGGS

Meat production in Malta constitutes breeding of animals strictly in farms since rearing of animals in fields is not possible due to lack of space and the small size of land parcels. Animals that are bred in Malta for meat production include rabbits, pigs, poultry, lamb and beef.

Rabbit breeding in Malta reflects the large local demand for this traditional meat, especially by restaurants specialising in fried and stewed rabbit. There are a large number of individuals who breed rabbits on a small scale, even for their own consumption or as a hobby. Nevertheless, there are around ten farms that breed rabbits on a commercial scale with over 300 breeding does. Such farms are equipped with modern rabbit housing and abide by hygiene regulations enforced by the Veterinary authorities.

Pig breeding in Malta is based on the local pig meat demand for which around 1,500 pigs are slaughtered every week. This demand is supplied from around 111 licensed farms that are organised under a pig producer cooperative that

sells whole pigs to processors, who then take care of transforming this particular livestock in deboned cuts or processed products such as Maltese sausages, ham cuts and bacon. There are around 6,000 sows (female pigs) in the local swine industry that are controlled by Veterinary regulations for animal welfare and hygiene. Pig breeding by unlicensed farms is strictly prohibited by Maltese law.

Poultry production in Malta is based on 80 broiler chicken farms and 30 egg laying hen farms. Broiler chickens are slaughtered in four licensed slaughtering lines and are supplied to butchers, supermarkets and food establishments all over the islands. This fresh product has to compete with frozen imports which are generally processed or pre-cooked. Eggs are delivered fresh from layer farms to supermarkets, groceries and food establishments on a daily basis. Nevertheless, there are some farmers who keep their own hens and produce eggs from cage-free hens. Other poultry products grown by licensed chicken breeders include turkeys, quails and *kapuċelli*, which are a small chicken breed that was traditionally bred in Malta and was lately re-introduced on the local market.

Lamb production is a by-product of sheep farmers who breed sheep for their milk and the production of ġbejniet. Lambs are raised for meat and for the use of their stomachs to extract rennet for ġbejniet production. Female lambs can also be kept in the herd for the production of milk. Lamb meat is traditionally eaten on Easter Sunday in the form of a stew to celebrate the end of the Lenten period.

Beef produced in Malta is generally grown on dairy farms as a secondary product to compliment milk production. Nevertheless, there are farms specialising in beef production for the local demand. Due to competition with imported high quality beef, the local industry is not extensive.

Typical meat product: *Zalzett tal-Malti*

A ubiquitous product found in butcher shops, supermarkets and groceries around the Maltese Islands is the Maltese pork sausage that is better known as *zalzett tal-Malti*. It can be bought fresh or dried and it is an important component of the Maltese cuisine. *Zalzett tal-Malti* can be eaten with ħobż biż-żejt, served with *galletti*, grilled, fried, stewed and steamed. Some like to eat it raw as well even if it is not recommended. *Zalzett tal-Malti* is made of pork, sea salt, coriander seeds, black peppercorns and parsley. A *zalzett*

tal-Malti version with reduced salt content and thinner skin is lately being sold, especially to be used for barbeques.

GRAPES AND WINES

In Malta, viticulture is one of the most ancient agricultural activities. The cultivation of vines has for centuries been of focal importance to inhabitants of the Maltese archipelago. Vines were traditionally planted in places where the soil was inferior, where there was no water supply and also in places where the farmer found it difficult to work the land such as on hill sides. A testimony of the historical link of vines with Malta is

the large number of grape varieties (over 120) that were present before phylloxera disease wiped out many vines all over Europe in the 18th century. From that point onwards, Maltese vines started being grafted onto American rootstocks that are resistant to the disease.

There are two indigenous vine varieties, Ġellewża and Girgentina, that produce large grape bunches in large quantities which are used both as fruit and for wine making. Around 60% of the vineyards in Malta are dedicated to these two indigenous varieties. There are about sixty international vine varieties in Malta that are exclusively used for wine making by twelve local wineries. The most popular varieties are Merlot, Syrah, Grenache, Cabernet Sauvignon and Cabernet Franc for red varieties, while the most common whites are Chardonnay, Vermentino, Viognier and Trebbiano. With EU accession, the Maltese consumer trend was to choose wines made from international grape varieties. Nevertheless, the *Ġellewża* variety is currently being given more importance and a number of *DOK Ġellewża* wines are also being produced.

The success of such a wealthy tradition stands to reason, given that our island has all the ingredients for the production of good quality wine. The Maltese climate improves the grape quality with a high sugar level and low acidity. In the last decade, there was an increase in the number of vine plantings from around 300 hectares to nearly 900 hectares.

Farmers and viticulturalists are making use of innovative planting techniques, pruning, as well as machinery used in the vineyard. This led to a large increase in the production of quality wines being classified as DOK and IGT. These wines are labelled by a banderole on wine bottles and must conform to both Maltese and EU legislation. These labels clearly show the denomination of the wine, the vintage year and also the origin. The total

wine production has increased to 21,000 hectolitres per year, with an average grape production of 2.92 million kilograms per year.

Typical grape product: Homemade wine

The traditional homemade Maltese wine is produced from *Ġellewża* (red) and *Girgentina* (white). These indigenous grapes are harvested in early September and mashed with the feet or using a manual grape masher. The grape is then left to ferment in a large container or barrel for three days, after which the juice is filtered into large globular glass containers called *damiġġani* that are sealed with cork and a narrow tube to permit fermentation. The leftovers of the grape must, composed of stalks and grape skin, are put back into the containers and mixed with water and sugar to create an inferior wine, called *tas-sekonda*. Wine in *damiġġani* is stored in a cool, dry place in a cellar or cave and left to mature until the feast of St Martin in November.

FRUIT TREES, STRAWBERRIES, MELONS AND WATERMELONS

Common fruit trees in Malta include peaches, figs, plums, Japanese medlars, grapes, nectarines, pomegranates, lemons, oranges, pears and *bambinella*. Summer is the main fruit season in Malta, starting from June until September. However, citrus trees produce like oranges and lemons are sold in the winter months. The total annual volume of fruit sold through official markets exceeds 5,600 tonnes.

A variety of delicious stone-fruits are grown in Malta including peaches, nectarines, apricots and plums. With the exception of the Japanese medlar that ripens in early May, all the other stone-fruits are harvested from late May until September. Traditional peach and nectarine varieties are nowadays being supplemented with locally grown international varieties that are farmed mostly in the agricultural area between Mġarr, Rabat and Siġġiewi. The best climatic conditions for a successful harvest include a cool winter so that fruit trees can hibernate, lack of wind in spring during the flowering period as well as long and sunny summer days for the fruits to ripen.

Apart from stone-fruits, the Maltese kitchen in summer is supplemented with delicious pears and *bambinelli.* The latter are typical Maltese miniature pears that are hard, juicy and give a typical reddish blush when ripe. Figs produced in Malta include *bajtar ta' San Ġwann, farkizzan* and *tin. Bajtar ta' San Ġwann* or St John's figs are the largest and first figs to ripen around the feast of St John the Baptist in late June. *Farkizzan* figs are small, bite size, black and pink figs that ripen in late July. *Tin* are medium sized figs that grow as a second crop on the same tree that produces *bajtar ta' San Ġwann* and ripen in August. *Bajtar tax-xewk* is another summer fruit that grows on prickly pear cactus and can vary from red to yellow or even orange spiny fruits.

The traditional small and exquisitely tasty Maltese strawberry has unfortunately disappeared from the market as it made way to larger varieties that are nowadays grown over a longer season. Strawberries are planted in September and start producing in November, but are in their full production from April until June. Due to its adaptability with food, milk, ice creams, sweets and desserts, the strawberry is one of the most favourite fruits in Malta. The Maltese sunny climate and soils seem to favour this fruit that is traditionally grown in the locality of Mġarr. The success of this fruit is manifested during the annual strawberry festival held in Mġarr in April that attracts thousands of locals and tourists alike. Red watermelons and yellow melons compliment the Maltese summer fruit season, especially in July and August.

In winter, citrus fruits that are harvested in the orchards around the Maltese Islands include the sweet orange, orange, red orange, grapefruit, tangerine and lemon.

The local sweet orange is perhaps the most widely requested fruit in the Christmas period for its characteristic scent and sweet flavour. The Maltese Islands can boast a large number of centenarian citrus orchards that were planted by the Knights of St John in the central part of Malta and in a number of valleys. Local citrus fruits are demanded fresh to be used for marmalades, juices, liqueurs, candied peel and even for medicinals and cosmetics.

Typical fruit product: Dried, and Stuffed dried figs

Dried figs, or as most commonly known *tin taċ-ċappa*, are a traditional staple food in the Maltese, rural, winter diet as a source of sugar intake during the cold months. Figs are picked in the cool summer morning, split in two and left to dry in the sun for a couple of days. The dried fruits are eventually pressed firmly into tin containers and stored in a dark

place to be consumed in winter. Bay laurel leaves, fennel seeds, cinnamon and anisette are added to each layer of pressed, dried figs.

Stuffed, dried figs are very popular and are usually served with coffee after a meal. They are the Maltese version of *petit fours*. Making dried figs takes time; so you can buy a packet of ready, dried figs. Then cut them in half and stuff with large pieces of walnuts. Sprinkle some icing sugar on top before serving. Needless to say, the taste will not be the same as those that are bought fresh and dried at home.

FRESH VEGETABLES

A range of vegetables are cultivated in Malta either as field crops or protected in greenhouses. In greenhouses, Maltese farmers cultivate tomatoes, cucumber, aubergines, zucchini, bell pepper, runner beans, lettuce as well as herbs. These vegetables are also grown as field crops requiring irrigation. Other field crops include potatoes, onions, garlic, kohlrabi, cauliflower, cabbages and broad beans. Cauliflowers, cabbages, lettuce and zucchini in Malta are cultivated nearly all year round. The total annual volume of vegetables sold through official markets averages around 40,000 tonnes.

Most tomatoes grown in the open fields are grown to supply three main processors of a traditional tomato paste known as *kunserva*. Besides this, there are also tomatoes produced for fresh table consumption. These can be grown using three different cultivation methods. There is the low plant cultivar method, the traditional vine method using reeds as support and the greenhouse method with rope support. The low plant cultivar method implies that tomato plants are grown without support as in the case of the tomatoes for processing. The vine method involves a structure of four reeds tied in the form of a pyramid that is used to support tomato plants. Greenhouse tomatoes are cultivated using extendable ropes that are dragged along a horizontal pivot to permit plant growth. Tomatoes produced in greenhouses have a longer harvesting season and supply the fresh market for most of the year.

A well-known Maltese vegetable is the potato. For decades, local famers have been exporting it to Northern countries that find it difficult to grow this product due to freezing winter temperatures. Spring potatoes in Malta are grown exclusively for export; to reach the early market in the Netherlands, Germany, Switzerland and UK. The winter potato crop, which is less popular among farmers, is grown only for the local market.

Typical vegetable product: Sun-dried tomatoes

The secret for high quality sun-dried tomatoes is that they must be freshly picked, ripe but firm. After picking, they are washed, dried and halved. Salt is sprinkled on the cut side and then put outside on trays to dry in the summer sun. The tomatoes shouldn't be left outside at night and should be taken out every morning so that the sun-drying process continues. Once the tomatoes are dry, they shrink and can be stored in glass jars, somewhere away from sunlight, in a cool and dry place. Sun-dried tomatoes are used in various recipes such as with *ħobż biż-żejt* and to compliment pasta dishes.

FISH

Notwithstanding the fact that the Maltese Islands are surrounded by the Mediterranean Sea, fish is not a prevailing source of food intake by locals. As a matter of fact, the fishing industry in Malta was traditionally very modest, seasonal, coastal and limited to a very small variety of fish. Today, fishing takes place all year round because of the increase in demand for fish, especially for the catering business. The total annual volume of fish landings in the main fishing ports averages 1,120,000 tonnes, but this varies from year to year. Maltese

consume around 7kg per year of fish per head, which is supplemented from local aquaculture and frozen fish imports.

Maltese fishing is described as being typically Mediterranean artisanal type, which caters for multiple species and uses multiple gear, with fishermen switching from one gear to another several times throughout the year. The source of revenue of local fishermen depends on the fresh sale of highly prized fish species that are caught by traditional artisanal methods during very short fishing trips. The local seafood variety contributes significantly to the upkeep of specialised restaurants, which coupled with the colourful traditional fishing vessels, add to the touristic assets of the Maltese archipelago.

In the months between April and July, the fish market is dominated by landings of bluefin tuna, with the second most plentiful species being the swordfish. The peak fishing period for swordfish is between May and August, but it is still targeted throughout the year. Landings of the renowned *lampuki* (dolphin fish) occur mainly between August and December. Other major species associated with this fishing season are pilot fish, amberjack and small bluefin tuna, which are caught as secondary species.

During the winter months of December to April, most boats target lucrative sea-bottom species before reverting to tuna long-lining, with catches of swordfish and albacore as secondary species. Landings of small, gregarious, surface and sea-bottom species are generally not seasonal, with bogue and mackerel being the most common species caught by traditional traps made out of cane strips (*nasses tal-vopi*). Prawns originate exclusively from trawling, which takes place throughout the year, with quantities reducing in winter months due to unfavourable weather.

Typical fish product: Salted fish

Various types of fish were traditionally preserved in salt as there was no refrigeration back then. Tuna, anchovy, mackerel, sardines and *lampuki* were amongst the favourite salted fish to be eaten with *ħobż biż-żejt* or cooked as a *stuffat* (stew) or with *aljotta* (the traditional local fish soup). The salting process includes chopping off the fish head, leaving the blood to drain off, filleting the raw fish, layering it in a jar, covering each layer in salt and leaving it to mature for a couple of weeks. The end product is undoubtedly extremely salty and thus a small portion at a time is consumed.

COFFEE

As in all other countries coffee is very popular in Malta. The modern way of brewing coffee is totally different from that of some years ago. According to tradition, the Maltese housewife used to brew coffee in a special coffee pot called *stanjata* on low heat for quite a long time. Special attention was needed; if the coffee over spilled then it was ruined. After it was brewed, it could not be drunk straight away; it had to be left for some time for the sediment to settle. Sometimes whole cloves were added to the ground coffee beans before brewing.

SHORTCRUST PASTRY

SHORTCRUST PASTRY

Shortcrust pastry is the most widely used type of pastry. It is perfect for sweet or savoury pies, tarts and quiches. When cooked, it has a light and crumbly texture that melts in the mouth. Many people will eat a slice of pie, tart or quiche just for the pastry's taste.

It is made with twice the amount of flour to fat and its texture largely depends on which type of fat is used and how it is integrated into the flour. Good pastry requires very little handling indeed; which sometimes can be quite tricky.

Below is some helpful information about the ingredients and techniques used to make 'perfect' shortcrust pastry.

1   When making shortcrust pastry, all necessary ingredients and utensils should be as cold as possible.

2   This applies mostly for the margarine. It should be cold, but not too cold that it becomes impossible to rub it into the flour. On the other hand, if it is too soft and warm, it will begin to melt and become oily; which will result in pastry that doesn't stay intact when it is being rolled out. The fat may become warm from taking too long to rub it into the flour; this could also happen if the fat is too cold.

3   For the best pastry results, you have to work quickly. Therefore, the temperature of the fat must be taken into consideration.

4   If you will be using egg yolks to bind the pastry, there will be no need for you to add water. If you use too much liquid, the pastry becomes tough.

5   Sieve the flour into a large bowl, holding the sieve as high as possible, so that the flour gets a really good airing.

6   Add the margarine, cut into smallish lumps, then begin to rub it into the flour using your fingertips only and being as light as possible.

7   As you gently rub the fat into the flour, lift it up high and let it fall back into the bowl, which again means that air is being incorporated all the time. Do this just long enough to make the mixture crumbly with a few odd lumps here and there.

8   Once the flour and fat mixture resembles breadcrumbs, sprinkle one or two tablespoons of water evenly over the flour mixture. If too much water is added, the pastry will turn into a sticky mess, making it almost impossible to roll out. However, if not enough water is added, the baked pastry will crumble and fall to pieces.

9   When making sweet shortcrust pastry, mix well together the sugar, egg yolk, vanilla essence and lemon rind in a separate

bowl. Add this mixture to the flour mixture before you start adding the water.

10   Once the liquid has been added, the mixture needs to be brought together to form a dough. To start with, the best method is by using a knife rather than your fingers since the pastry should be handled as little as possible.

11   Work the knife using cutting and stirring motions; the mixture should start to come together. Finish off by pressing the ingredients together with your fingers, adding more water if necessary, until the bowl has been completely cleaned and a nice and smooth ball of dough has been formed.

12   It is really important to give the pastry a rest before rolling it out, so that the gluten in the flour has enough time to react with the water and gain elasticity, which will render rolling the pastry out that much easier.

13   Wrap the pastry dough ball in stretch and seal and place it in the refrigerator for a minimum of 30 minutes. You can prepare it overnight and leave it in the fridge.

14   When you remove the pastry from the refrigerator, let it stand for a while to bring it back up to room temperature before rolling; when it softens up, the pastry is more manageable.

15   Make sure that the surface on which you are going to roll out the pastry dough is clean and dry. Lightly dust the surface with flour and do the same with the rolling pin.

16   Roll the pastry out to the desired thickness and shape for the recipe that you are following.

SAVOURY SHORTCRUST PASTRY

GĦAĠINA GĦAT-TORTI

420g plain flour
180g margarine
8g salt
112g cold water

SWEET SHORTCRUST PASTRY

GĦAĠINA GĦAT-TORTI ĦELWIN

480g plain flour
300g margarine
120g sugar
2 eggs
grated rind of 1 lemon
vanilla essence

SOUPS

CLEAR BEEF SOUP

BRODU TAĊ-ĊANGA

1l water
500g beef shin
75g carrots
50g onions
50g tomato paste
celery
salt and pepper

1   Peel and slice the onions and carrots. Wash and cut the celery into medium sized pieces.

2   Put the vegetables in a medium sized pan and cover them with water. Add the tomato paste and beef shin.

3   Put the pan on a medium flame and bring it to a boil.

4   Lower the heat and leave the soup to simmer for about 1½ hours, skimming regularly.

5   Add salt and pepper to taste and serve hot.

TRIPE MINESTRONE

MINESTRA BIL-KIRXA

1½l water or stock
500g tripe
200g carrots
200g pumpkin
150g onions
150g dried peas
150g potatoes
150g cauliflower
50g tomato paste
celery
salt and pepper

Soak the peas overnight.

Clean the tripe, cut it into small pieces and wash it in plenty of salted water.

Rewash the tripe. Fill a saucepan with water and boil the tripe for about 45 minutes.

Peel, wash and chop all the vegetables into small pieces. Put them in a large pan.

Add the peas, water or stock, tomato paste and tripe. Bring to a boil.

Lower the flame and simmer for 1½ hours.

Add seasoning and serve hot.

MEAT BALLS SOUP

SOPPA BIL-PULPETTI TAL-LAĦAM

1l water

400g minced meat... use either pork or beef or a mixture of both

100g onions

100g carrots

50g celery

50g semolina

1 egg

chopped parsley

seasoning

1 Wash, peel and dice all the vegetables in small pieces.

2 Prepare a pan with water. Bring it to a boil and add all the vegetables.

3 Place the minced meat in a bowl. Add the egg, parsley and seasoning. Mix everything well.

4 Sprinkle the semolina either on a flat plate or on a piece of greaseproof paper. Shape the meat mixture in small balls. Coat each ball with semolina.

5 Add the meat balls to the soup and continue cooking for a further 40 minutes.

6 Check seasoning and serve immediately.

KUSKSU WITH BROAD BEANS

KUSKSU BIL-FUL

1l water or stock
400g broad beans
200g onions
200g kusksu (see note below)
25g tomato paste
grated cheese
a knob of margarine
garlic
salt and freshly ground pepper

1   Peel and chop finely the onions and garlic.

2   Melt the margarine in a large casserole and lightly fry the chopped onions and garlic until they obtain a golden colour.

3   Skin the beans from both sides.

4   Put the skinned beans in a pan with plenty of water. Bring to a boil, lower the heat and continue cooking until the beans are tender.

5   Add the tomato paste, beans and water to the onions and garlic.

6   Add the kusksu and continue simmering for about 12 minutes.

7   Season with salt and pepper and serve with plenty of grated cheese on top.

Kusksu is different from the couscous which is a typical Arabic dish. Kusksu is made of round, small pasta which is a little bigger than a coriander in size. Instead of broad beans, peas may be used. You can add a soft cheeselet as well.

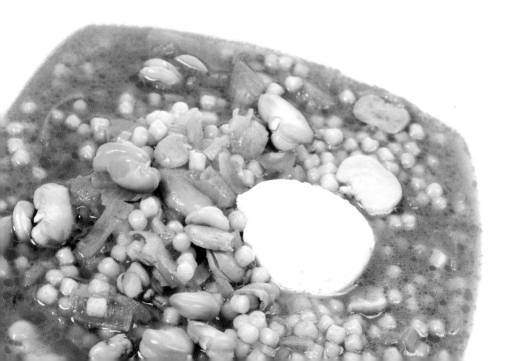

PUMPKIN SOUP

SOPPA TAL-QARGĦA ĦAMRA

1l beef stock (or water
and beef bones)
200g pumpkin, chopped
75g onions, chopped
25g butter or margarine
parsley, chopped
salt and pepper

Melt the margarine or butter in a saucepan, add the onions and soften them for about 8 minutes. Now add the chopped pumpkin, give everything a good stir and season with salt and pepper.

Put the lid on and, keeping the heat low, allow the vegetables to sweat gently and release their juices.

Pour in the stock and simmer gently for about 1 hour.

When the soup is ready, pour it into a food processor or blender and blend to a purée, leaving a little bit of texture – it doesn't need to be absolutely smooth.

Serve the soup in warm bowls with chopped parsley sprinkled over the top.

WIDOW'S SOUP

SOPPA TAL-ARMLA

This is a traditional dish. Its name originates from the fact that the ingredients used for this dish, upon being inexpensive, were affordable even by the 'poor' widow.

200g ricotta
150g peeled tomatoes
125g peas
125g cauliflower
100g onions
100g potatoes
50g tomato paste
4 eggs
seasoning
frying oil

1   Wash, peel and cut all the vegetables in very small pieces. Place them in different bowls.

2   Pour some oil in a medium sized pan and heat. When hot, quickly fry the onions, stirring all the time. Don't brown.

3   Add the cauliflower, tomato paste and chopped tomatoes and continue cooking for a few more minutes, stirring all the time.

4   Put this mixture in a saucepan. Add the water, peas, potatoes and seasoning. Mix well. Place on a medium flame until the mixture boils.

5   Lower the heat and simmer until the vegetables are cooked.

6   Add the eggs one by one. Cut the ricotta into four pieces and add the ricotta pieces to the soup. Continue cooking for 5 minutes.

7   Serve piping hot. When serving, put a piece of ricotta and one egg in each plate.

THICK VEGETABLE SOUP

MINESTRA

1¼l water
100g pumpkin
100g cauliflower
100g carrots
50g white onions
25g celery
25g grated cheese
25g tomato paste
25g pasta
grated cheese
seasoning
frying oil

1   Wash, peel and cut all the vegetables in very small pieces. Place them in different bowls.

2   Pour some oil in a medium sized pan and heat. When hot, fry the onions until tender, stirring all the time. Don't brown.

3   Put this mixture in a saucepan. Add the water, all vegetables and seasoning. Mix well. Put on a medium flame until the mixture boils.

4   Lower the heat and continue cooking until all the vegetables are cooked.

5   Meanwhile, cook some short pasta. The pasta should be half cooked.

6   Add the pasta to the soup 20 minutes before serving and check seasoning. Mix well. Continue cooking on a very low flame, stirring frequently.

7   Serve immediately with plenty of grated cheese on top.

VEGETABLE SOUP WITH PORK

KAWLATA

2l water
200g pork belly
100g cauliflower
100g carrots
100g cabbage
100g potatoes
75g pumpkin
50g white onions
50g celery
50g bacon
20g tomato paste
short pasta
salt and pepper
frying oil

1   Wash, peel and cut all the vegetables in very small pieces. Place them in different bowls.

2   Pour some oil in a medium sized pan and heat. When hot, quickly fry the onions, stirring all the time. Don't brown.

3   Add the chopped vegetables and continue cooking for a few more minutes, stirring all the time.

4   Add the water and tomato paste. Bring to a boil.

5   Lower the heat and add the pork belly together with the bacon cut in cubes. Simmer for 1½ hours.

6   Meanwhile, cook some short pasta. The pasta should be half cooked.

7   Add the pasta to the soup 20 minutes before serving. Add seasoning and mix well. Continue cooking on a very low flame, stirring frequently.

8   Serve immediately.

FISH SOUP

ALJOTTA

1l water
500g white fish
100g leeks
75g peeled tomatoes
3 garlic cloves
chopped parsley
chopped mint
boiled rice
1 tbsp freshly squeezed lemon juice
salt and pepper

1   Wash and slice the leeks. Peel and chop the garlic cloves.

2   Put the garlic and leeks into a pan and add the water and lemon juice.

3   Clean the fish, remove the bones and place it in a pan. If desired, you can put the fish in a muslin bag, fasten it securely and immerse it in the pan. When cooked, you can easily remove the muslin bag from the pan.

4   Wash and slice the tomatoes and add them to the pan, together with the chopped parsley and mint. Cook on low heat for 35 minutes.

5   Boil some rice while the soup is cooking.

6   When the soup is ready, pass it through a sieve to make sure that there are no fish bones left.

7   Before serving, season with salt and pepper and add small pieces of fish.

8   Serve hot with boiled rice.

PASTA & RICE

SPAGHETTI WITH TOMATO SAUCE

SPAGETTI BIZ-ZALZA TAT-TADAM

400g spaghetti
400g tomatoes
100g onions
50g tomato paste
30ml water
olive oil
garlic
basil
grated Parmesan cheese
salt and freshly ground pepper

1   Peel and chop the tomatoes. Peel and finely chop the onions and garlic.

2   Heat the olive oil in a saucepan and fry the onions and garlic until golden brown.

3   Add the water, tomatoes, tomato paste, basil, salt and pepper. Bring the mixture to a boil, reduce the heat and simmer gently for 30 minutes or until thickened.

4   While the sauce is simmering, cook the spaghetti in a large pan of boiling, salted water until just tender. Drain, place in a serving bowl and keep hot.

5   Check to see if the sauce needs more seasoning.

6   Pour the sauce over the spaghetti and serve immediately with plenty of grated cheese on top.

When fresh tomatoes are cheap and plentiful, use 500g peeled and chopped fresh instead of canned tomatoes and 1 tablespoon tomato paste.

SPAGHETTI WITH BACON SAUCE

SPAGETTI BIZ-ZALZA TAL-BEJKEN

400g spaghetti
400g peeled tomatoes
200g bacon cubes
fresh sage leaves
olive oil
salt and freshly ground pepper

1   Peel and chop the tomatoes and put them in a small bowl.

2   Heat some olive oil in a deep frying pan and fry the bacon until golden in colour.

3   Add the chopped tomatoes to the bacon and mix well.

4   Add the sage leaves, salt and pepper. Continue cooking on low heat for a further 10 minutes.

5   Meanwhile, boil the spaghetti in plenty of salted water.

6   When cooked, drain and place in the pan with sauce. Cook for a further 2 minutes making sure that all the spaghetti cords are coated with sauce.

7   Serve immediately.

SPAGHETTI WITH RABBIT SAUCE

SPAGETTI BIZ-ZALZA TAL-FENEK

500g spaghetti

300g rabbit meat

300g tomato juice

200g onions

150g garden peas... if using frozen ones, follow the directions given on packet

50g tomato paste

5 or 6 garlic cloves... add as much as desired

1 glass red wine

grated cheese

margarine

bay leaves

rabbit seasoning

salt and freshly ground pepper

1   Peel and finely chop the onions and garlic cloves. Chop the rabbit meat in medium sized cubes. If you have a whole rabbit, clean it thoroughly and add the head and liver to the sauce.

2   Melt the margarine in a well heated saucepan. Fry the onions and garlic until transparent. Add the rabbit meat and fry until brown all over. Lower the heat and add the rabbit seasoning and tomato paste. Continue cooking for about 5 minutes.

3   Add the wine, tomato juice and bay leaves. Sprinkle some salt and freshly ground pepper. Bring to a boil and simmer for about 20 minutes. Add the peas and continue cooking, always on very low heat, for another 20 minutes. Check occasionally to see that the sauce doesn't dry up.

4   Meanwhile, boil the spaghetti. Drain well and pour the rabbit sauce on top.

5   Serve while very hot with a side dish of grated cheese.

 The rabbit seasoning can be found in most butcher shops and supermarkets. It gives rabbit stew that extra special flavour.

SPAGHETTI WITH OCTOPUS SAUCE

SPAGETTI BIZ-ZALZA TAL-QARNIT

800g octopus
800g spaghetti
200g onions
200g tomatoes
150g peas
100g black olives
75g tomato paste
300ml red wine
a mixture of fresh basil and fresh mint
olive oil
lemon zest
salt and freshly ground pepper

1   Cut the octopus into even sized pieces and put them in a small bowl.

2   Heat a small quantity of oil and water in a large and deep frying pan and fry the octopus pieces. Remove them from over the heat when cooked and leave to cool for about 15 minutes.

3   Add the tomato paste and herbs and continue cooking.

4   Peel and finely chop the onions and fry them in a little oil.

5   Peel and chop the tomatoes and add them to the onions.

6   Slice the olives and add them, together with the lemon zest, to the tomato mixture. Mix well.

7   Mix this mixture with the octopus mixture. Add the peas, wine and seasoning. Continue cooking for about 30 minutes.

8   Meanwhile, boil the spaghetti in plenty of salted water. Drain well when ready.

9   Serve the octopus sauce on top of the cooked spaghetti.

VERMICELLI WITH EGGS

FROĠA TAT-TARJA

This is the Maltese version of the Italian pasta omelette. Ideally, it should be made with fine pasta, but you can use any type of leftover pasta. Ricotta and fresh Maltese cheeslets are sometimes included.

250g vermicelli (the finest of spaghetti)

50g butter

25g grated cheese

3 eggs

salt and freshly ground pepper

1   Boil the *vermicelli* in plenty of salted water. Drain once ready.

2   Beat the eggs in a mixing bowl and add the cheese. If you will be using ricotta or fresh cheeselets, add them now and mix well.

3   Mix the pasta with the egg mixture and stir well. Season with some salt and freshly ground pepper.

4   Heat the butter in a frying pan.

5   Fry the pasta mixture. When it has set firmly enough, turn it so that it can finish cooking on the other side. When lightly golden on its bottom side, lift the pasta omelette out and serve immediately.

PASTA WITH RICOTTA

GĦAĠIN BL-IRKOTTA

600g pasta
400g ricotta
50g butter
5 eggs
chopped parsley
grated cheese
freshly grated nutmeg
salt and freshly ground pepper

1   Boil the pasta in plenty of salted water. Drain well when cooked.

2   Put the ricotta in a large mixing bowl. Add the eggs, freshly grated nutmeg and seasoning. Mix well until the mixture is of a creamy consistency. Add the chopped parsley and mix well.

3   Heat the butter in a large pan and add the pasta. Cook for a few minutes, stirring all the time.

4   Add the ricotta mixture and continue cooking for about 20 minutes, always on a very low flame. Stir frequently while taking care so as not to break the pasta.

5   Serve immediately with plenty of grated cheese on top.

STUFFED LUMACONI

BEBBUX MIMLI

400g lumaconi (snail shaped large pasta)

300g ricotta… some of it can be substituted by fresh Maltese cheeselets

50g semolina

50g grated cheese

2 eggs

tomato sauce

finely chopped parsley

freshly grated nutmeg

salt and freshly ground pepper

1   Put the ricotta in a large mixing bowl. Add the eggs, freshly grated nutmeg, some of the grated cheese and seasoning. Mix well until the mixture is of a creamy consistency. Add the chopped parsley and mix well.

2   Fill the *lumaconi* with the ricotta mixture. Place the stuffed pasta shapes on a large, flat plate.

3   Fill a large pan with water and heat until it starts boiling.

4   Sprinkle the semolina on a flat plate or a piece of greaseproof paper. Dip the ricotta side of the *lumaconi* in the semolina. By doing so the *lumaconi* will remain intact during cooking.

5   When the water is boiling, add some salt and, with great care, start cooking the *lumaconi*.

6   Heat the tomato sauce in the meantime.

7   Cooked *lumaconi* will rise to the water's surface. Paying special attention not to scald yourself, carefully remove them from the water.

8   Place the *lumaconi* in a large serving dish and spread the tomato sauce over them.

9   Sprinkle the rest of the grated cheese and some freshly ground pepper on top.

10   Serve immediately.

RAVIOLI

RAVJUL

For the pastry

250g semolina
200g flour
pinch of salt
water for binding

For the filling

200g ricotta
2 eggs
finely chopped parsley
salt and freshly ground pepper

For the topping

tomato sauce
grated cheese
salt and freshly ground pepper

1   Sift the flour in a large mixing bowl. Add the semolina and some salt. Start adding water carefully and knead until you have a smooth and elastic dough.

2   Wrap the dough in stretch and seal or put it in a plastic bag. Leave it to rest for at least 1 hour. You can prepare the dough the day before and leave it overnight in the fridge.

3   Put the ricotta and eggs in a mixing bowl. Mix well until the mixture is of a creamy consistency. Add the chopped parsley and seasoning and mix again.

4   Place the dough on a lightly floured surface. Divide it into 4 pieces.

5   Roll each piece into long strips about 8cm wide. Dampen the edges with water.

6   Put small balls of ricotta mixture some 2cm from the pastry's edge, 4cm apart.

7   Turn one edge of the pastry on the other one and press to seal. Using a ravioli cutter, cut out the pastry 10cm away from the filling.

8   Place the ravioli on a large plate dusted with semolina and leave them to rest for about 10 minutes.

9   Bring a large saucepan of water to a boil. Add the ravioli and cook for 4-6 minutes until *al dente*. Drain.

10   Meanwhile, heat the tomato sauce. Pour it upon the ravioli.

11   Serve immediately with grated cheese and seasoning sprinkled on top.

BAKED MACARONI IN PASTRY

TIMPANA

800g shortcrust pastry
400g pasta… use either penne or macaroni
200g minced meat… use either one type of meat like beef or pork or a mixture of both
200g chopped tomatoes
120g chopped onions
60g grated cheese… choose good quality tasting cheese like Grana Padano or Parmesan
40g tomato paste
3 eggs
garlic
oil
sesame seeds
salt and freshly ground pepper

1   Boil the pasta in plenty of salted water. Cool the cooked pasta under running water and strain.

2   Heat some oil in a large frying pan and fry the onions and garlic. Add the minced meat and continue cooking on low heat for about 8 minutes.

3   Add the tomato paste and chopped fresh tomatoes. Continue cooking on low heat for a further 20 minutes.

4   Preheat the oven 190°C, gas mark 5.

5   Put the pasta either in a large bowl or in the same pan where you boiled it. Add the meat sauce, eggs, seasoning and cheese. Mix well, taking great care so as not to break the pasta.

6   Line a pie dish with pastry. Fill it with the pasta mixture and cover again with pastry.

7   Egg wash, sprinkle some sesame seeds on top and cook in the medium to hot oven for about 50 minutes.

BAKED RICE

ROSS FIL-FORN

250g rice

250g minced meat… use either pork or beef or a mixture of both

200g onions

150g tomatoes

150g grated cheese

30g tomato paste

300ml stock

4 eggs, lightly beaten

garlic cloves… use as much as desired

basil leaves

oil

seasoning

1   Peel and finely chop the onions and garlic. Peel and chop the tomatoes in large pieces. Put them in a separate bowl.

2   Heat some oil in a large, deep saucepan and quickly fry the onions and garlic, stirring frequently. The onions and garlic should just begin to change colour.

3   Lower the heat. Add the minced meat and continue cooking for some more minutes until the meat is almost cooked. Add the chopped tomatoes, tomato paste and basil leaves. Mix well and cook for a couple of minutes.

4   Add the stock, cover the saucepan and simmer for about 30 minutes.

5   Preheat the oven 180°C, gas mark 4.

6   Boil the rice in plenty of salted water. Strain the cooked rice well and cool it under running water.

7   Add the rice to the tomato and meat sauce. Mix well. Add the beaten eggs and grated cheese. Leave some cheese for the top. Add some freshly ground pepper and some salt.

8   Lightly grease a baking dish and place the rice mixture in it. Level the top and sprinkle the rest of the grated cheese over it. Add some more pepper if desired.

9   Bake for about 40-45 minutes and serve immediately.

BAKED MACARONI

IMQARRUN FIL-FORN

This is one of the most popular Maltese dishes. It is like *timpana*, but without the pastry. In most families, it is the main dish on Sundays.

400g macaroni

400g minced meat... use either pork or beef or a mixture of both

200g tomatoes

100g onions

50g tomato paste

50g grated cheese

60ml beef stock

3 eggs

2 hard boiled eggs

oil

milk

garlic

basil

salt and freshly ground pepper

1   Peel and finely chop the onions and garlic.

2   Peel and chop the tomatoes and hard boiled eggs.

3   Heat some oil in a large frying pan and quickly fry the onions and garlic until golden brown. Add the minced meat and continue frying for about 10 minutes on a high flame.

4   Lower the heat. Add the tomatoes, basil, seasoning, tomato paste and stock and simmer for a further 30 minutes. This sauce can be prepared overnight since it freezes very well.

5   Preheat the oven 190°C, gas mark 5.

6   Lightly grease a baking dish.

7   Meanwhile, fill a large pot with water, bring it to a boil and cook the pasta until *al dente*. Drain and put the pasta in a large mixing bowl.

8   Pour the meat sauce over the pasta and stir well.

9   Add the eggs, milk, grated cheese, hard boiled eggs and seasoning. Stir well while making sure that you don't break the macaroni.

10   Put the pasta mixture in the baking dish. Bake for around 45 minutes or until it is firm and the top has turned crispy.

MEAT & POULTRY

PORK AND POTATO CASSEROLE

CASSEROLE TAL-MAJJAL U PATATA

500g pork
400g peeled potatoes
300g onions
3 or 4 garlic heads
red chilli pepper
fennel seeds
seasoning

1   Preheat the oven 170°C, gas mark 3.

2   Remove the skin and extra fat from the pork and cut it in small cubes.

3   Peel and chop the onions and garlic. Heat some oil in a frying pan and quickly fry them, turning frequently.

4   Add the pork cubes and continue cooking until the pork is cooked from the outside.

5   Cut the potatoes in large wedges and add them to the pork. Mix well. Add the whole chilli pepper and continue cooking for a further 5 minutes.

6   Add the seasoning and fennel seeds. Mix well and put the mixture into a casserole. Add some water.

7   Cover and cook in the oven for about 90 minutes at a temperature varying between 150°C to 170°C, gas mark 2-3.

PORK STEW

STUFFAT TAL-MAJJAL

600g pork... opt for the best cuts taken from leg or shoulder

400g potatoes

300g onions

200g carrots

100g bacon

50g flour

50g margarine

1 glass white wine

water

celery

garlic cloves

chilli pepper (optional)

seasoning

1   Remove any fat and skin from the pork and cut it into medium sized cubes. Chop the bacon in small pieces.

2   Peel and finely chop the onions and garlic cloves.

3   Melt the margarine in a large saucepan and quickly fry the onions and garlic until they turn transparent.

4   Add the pork cubes and bacon and continue cooking, stirring continually. Lower the heat, add the flour and seasoning and continue cooking for about 8 minutes.

5   Peel and cut the vegetables into cubes. If the celery is not very tender, then you have to remove the outer part.

6   Add the chilli pepper, if desired, and wine. Stir thoroughly, taking care not to break the pork cubes. Lower the heat and cook for 5 minutes.

7   Add the water and vegetables. Bring the stew to a boil and simmer for 50 minutes. Instead of simmering it on top of the stove, you can place the pork stew in a casserole and cook it in a preheated oven 150°C, gas mark 2. Either way you cook it, check frequently to see that it doesn't dry up.

OVEN BAKED PORK CHOPS, MALTESE STYLE

KUSTILJI TAL-MAJJAL FIL-FORN, STIL MALTI

Maltese pork is renowned both for its succulent flavour as well as for its pinkish colour. No wonder that pork meat is eaten in almost all households! The most popular cuts are chops. These can be cooked in various ways: grilled, baked, pan fried or barbequed. Normally, chutney or mustard are served with pork chops instead of sauce or gravy.

This recipe is quite simple to prepare, but the end result is something exceptionally tasteful! With the help of the sage, garlic and juices of the pork, the potatoes acquire such a mouth-watering taste that they are by far even more desirable to eat than the baked pork chops themselves!

4 pork chops

1kg potatoes

300g onions

4 or 5 garlic cloves

olive oil

water

fennel seeds

salt and freshly ground pepper

1   Preheat the oven 180°C-190°C, gas mark 4-5.

2   Peel and thickly slice the onions and potatoes. Peel and chop the garlic in medium sized pieces. Remove the skin and extra fat from the pork chops.

3   Place a layer of onions and potatoes on the bottom of a large baking dish.

4   Put the pork chops on top. Sprinkle with garlic, salt and freshly ground pepper.

5   Cover the pork chops with the remaining potatoes and onions. Add some more seasoning and sprinkle the fennel seeds on top. Pour some oil and water. Always add the water from the side of the dish so that the herbs used as seasoning are not washed away.

6   Roast in the medium to hot oven for about 60 minutes. For the first 25 minutes, cover the dish with tin foil. After that, remove the foil so that the potatoes will eventually become crusty and golden brown.

ROAST SHOULDER OF PORK

SPALLA TAL-MAJJAL FIL-FORN

boneless shoulder of pork, skin on

600ml water or vegetable stock

2 onions, halved

2 carrots, peeled and halved lengthwise

2 sticks of celery, halved

1 head of garlic

6-8 fresh bay leaves

salt and freshly ground black pepper

1   Preheat the oven 220°C, gas mark 7.

2   Place the pork on a clean kitchen table, skin-side upwards. With a small, sharp knife make scores about a centimetre apart through the skin into the fat, but not so deep that you cut into the meat. The closer together you make the scores, the crisper and easier it will be to carve and serve the crackling. If the joint is tied, try not to cut through the string.

3   Rub salt right into all the scores you have just made, pulling the skin a little apart if you need to. Brush any excess salt off the surface and turn it over. Season the pork's underside with some salt and pepper.

4   Put the pork, skin-side up, in a roasting dish and place it in the preheated oven. Add the water or vegetable stock.

5   Roast for 30 minutes until the pork's skin starts to puff up and begins to turn into crackling. At this point, turn the heat down to 180°C, gas mark 4 and roast for another 30 minutes. Take the pork out of the oven and baste it with the fat in the bottom of the tray.

6   Carefully lift the pork up and transfer it to a plate.

7   Add all the vegetables, garlic and bay leaves to the tray and stir them into the fat.

8   Place the pork back on top of everything and return it to the oven to roast for another hour.

9   By this time the pork should be meltingly soft and tender. Move it very carefully to a serving dish, cover it with tin foil and leave it to rest for about 30 minutes before carving.

ROASTED LEMON PORK FILLET

FLETT TAL-MAJJAL FIL-FORN BIL-LUMI

pork fillet
juice of 2 lemons
2 tbsp honey
1 tbsp sesame seeds
grated zest of a lime
some margarine
seasoning

1. Preheat the oven 190°C, gas mark 5.

2. Trim any extra fat from the pork and pat it dry using kitchen paper.

3. Season well.

4. Brush the pork fillet with lemon juice.

5. Place the honey, sesame seeds, lime zest and margarine in a bowl. Mix well until all ingredients blend completely.

6. Coat the pork fillet with this mixture.

7. Place the pork fillet into a roasting dish and bake it for about 50 minutes.

8. Either serve hot with roast potatoes or cold with salad.

HONEY ROASTED PORK LOIN

KUSTILJI TAL-MAJJAL FIL-FORN BL-GĦASEL

2kg boneless pork loin
60g brown sugar
4 tbsp Maltese honey
2 tbsp mustard
carrots
onions
cloves
olive oil
cinnamon

1. Preheat the oven to 200°C, gas mark 6.

2. Wash and scrape the carrots and cut them into thick slices. Peel the onions and cut them into thick slices. Put the carrots and onions in a roasting dish.

3. Season the pork and place it on top of the carrots and onions.

4. Place the honey, mustard, cloves, cinnamon, sugar and oil in a bowl. Mix well until all the ingredients blend together.

5. Pour some of this mixture over the pork.

6. Add some water to the dish. Cover the whole dish with aluminium foil and bake in the hot oven for at least 90 minutes.

7. Baste frequently.

8. Remove the foil and pour the rest of the mixture over the pork.

9. Continue cooking for at least 45 more minutes.

10. Allow the pork to relax for about 30 minutes before carving.

STUFFED PORK

MAJJAL MIMLI

The pork used for this recipe should be boneless. Cuts can be taken from the shoulder, belly, loin or flank.

2kg pork
500g minced pork
300g minced beef
100g grated cheese
3 eggs
seasoning

1   Don't trim all the fat from the pork as this will help to keep it moist. Slice it in half lengthwise, batter the 2 halves with a rolling pin to flatten and widen them slightly, then season them with salt and freshly milled pepper.

2   Preheat the oven 200°C, gas mark 6.

3   Place the minced meat in a bowl and mix well. Add the seasoning, cheese and eggs. Mix until all the ingredients blend well together.

4   Stuff the pork with this mixture. Either wrap the pork in foil or ask your butcher to provide you with a baking net.

5   Continue cooking using the same method as for 'Roast Pork' (see page 82).

6   If you want pork crackling, you have to cut deep slits into the skin, using a sharp knife. This has to be done before you cook the meat.

7   Don't baste the pork during cooking or the crackling won't be crisp.

8   Remove the dish from the oven 35 minutes before cooking time. Great care should be taken while doing this since the hot gravy might scald you.

9   Remove the foil and continue cooking the pork on a higher temperature.

CHICKEN VEGETABLE CASSEROLE

CASSEROLE TAT-TIĠIEĠ U ĦAXIX

whole chicken
800ml stock
200g onions
200g cauliflower
200g broccoli
200g carrots
200g potatoes
50g flour
50g margarine
2 glasses red wine
garlic
fresh sage
seasoning

1   Preheat the oven 170°C, gas mark 3.

2   Cut the chicken in 8 pieces, season and quickly roast it in the oven until golden brown in colour.

3   Peel and chop the onions and garlic.

4   Melt the margarine in a large frying pan and lightly fry the onions, garlic and sage. Stir frequently because they shouldn't brown.

5   Wash, peel and dice all the remaining vegetables. Add them to the onion mixture and continue cooking for a few minutes.

6   Sprinkle the flour on top. Mix well and add the wine and stock.

7   Continue cooking until the mixture starts to boil, stirring frequently. Add the cooked chicken pieces and season.

8   Cook over high heat until the mixture boils, then reduce the heat to a low simmer and continue cooking for a further 80 minutes. Stir frequently.

9   Alternatively, cook in the oven 150°C-170°C, gas mark 2-3. Check frequently so that there is always liquid in the casserole.

STUFFED CHICKEN BROTH

TIĠIEĠA MIMLIJA FIL-BRODU

1 chicken of 1¼kg
300g minced pork
300g minced beef
200g onions
100g marrows
100g chopped ham
100g potatoes
100g carrots
2 eggs, lightly beaten
2 hard boiled eggs, chopped in small pieces
fresh parsley, finely chopped
celery
seasoning

1   Clean the chicken thoroughly inside and out with water and then pat dry with a paper towel.

2   In a large mixing bowl mix together the minced meats, hard boiled eggs, parsley, beaten eggs, chopped ham and seasoning. Mix well so that all the ingredients are well blended.

3   Once the stuffing has been thoroughly mixed together, loosely fill the neck and body cavities by spooning the stuffing mixture into these areas.

4   It is crucial that the body cavity is loosely filled with stuffing and not packed tight, as the stuffing will increase during cooking as juices from the meat are absorbed. Too much stuffing could prevent the poultry meat from being properly and thoroughly cooked.

5   After stuffing the chicken, truss it so that the stuffing does not come out during cooking.

6   Wash and chop the marrows and celery. Wash, peel and chop the potatoes, onions and carrots.

7   Fill a large pan with water and put on a high heat till it starts boiling. Add the chopped vegetables and cook, always on a high heat, for about 10 minutes.

8   Lower the heat. Add the chicken. Cover the pan with a lid and continue until the chicken is cooked.

9   Remove the chicken from the broth. Put into a roasting dish. Pat dry with paper towels and brush some olive oil on the chicken. Cook in a hot oven until you get a nice golden colour.

10   The broth should be served hot whilst the chicken can be served either hot or cold.

ROASTED FRESH LEG OF LAMB

KOXXA TAL-ĦARUF FIL-FORN

Fresh lamb is a Maltese delicacy widely cooked for Easter lunch. Two methods concerning its typical preparation are being given below. In the second instance, the flavour of cooked potatoes is something that cannot be described! Locally, it is not customary to serve mint sauce with lamb.

fresh leg of lamb
fresh rosemary
butter or olive oil
seasoning

Method 1

1   Simply rub some butter or oil on the leg and season with salt, pepper and fresh rosemary.

2   Roast in the same way as pork or beef.

3   Serve hot with gravy and potatoes.

Method 2

1   Prepare a quantity of sliced potatoes, onions and garlic and put them in the bottom of a baking dish.

2   Season well and place the lamb on top of the vegetables.

3   Roast in the same way as pork or beef.

ROAST LAMB

ḤARUF FIL-FORN

*lamb joint... can be either
leg or shoulder*

3 or 4 garlic cloves

1 tbsp extra virgin olive oil

fresh rosemary

*salt and freshly ground
pepper*

1   Peel the garlic and place it in a bowl. Add some salt and crush them together to a purée. Add the oil, chopped fresh rosemary and some freshly ground pepper. Mix well until all the ingredients blend together.

2   Preheat the oven 190°C, gas mark 5.

3   Spread a large sheet of foil over a roasting dish, place the lamb joint on it and make several small and deep holes in its fleshy parts with a skewer.

4   Spread the rosemary mixture all over the lamb's upper surface. Spread it as evenly as possible. Bring the foil's edges up over the lamb, make a pleat in the top and scrunch in the ends. This foil parcel should be fairly loose to allow the air to circulate.

5   Put the dish in the oven and bake the lamb for 2 hours, then open out the foil, baste the joint well with the juices and return it to the oven for a further 30 minutes to brown.

6   The above cooking time should result in lamb meat which is very slightly pink; you can cook it for more or less time, according to your taste.

7   Remove the cooked lamb from the oven and allow it to rest for 20 minutes before carving.

8   Serve with jacket potatoes or vegetables.

RABBIT STEW

STUFFAT TAL-FENEK

You can either buy a whole rabbit and cut it into pieces yourself or you can buy rabbit joints. You have to keep in mind that you have to serve 2 joints per person.

1 rabbit

200g onions

200g peas

200g tomatoes

40g tomato paste

3 garlic cloves

2 glasses red wine

½ tsp mixed spices

sage

bay leaves

seasoning

olives

olive oil

1   Peel and chop the tomatoes, onions and garlic in small pieces. Put them in separate bowls.

2   Pour the wine in a large bowl and add the sage, bay leaves and seasoning. Don't use all the wine, sage and bay leaves. Mix the ingredients well together. Place the rabbit joints in this marinade and leave to marinate for not more than 1 hour.

3   Meanwhile, heat some oil in a large saucepan and fry the onions and garlic. Stir frequently. They shouldn't brown. Lower the heat. Add the tomato paste, tomatoes, mixed spice, bay leaves and wine set aside, peas and some water. Cover the pan until the mixture reaches boiling point. If using frozen peas, follow the instructions on the packet before adding them to the mixture. When the mixture starts to boil, remove it from the heat.

4   Remove the rabbit joints from the marinade and pat them dry with kitchen paper. Pass the marinade through a sieve and set it aside.

5   Season the rabbit joints. Heat some oil in a sauté pan and fry them to a golden colour. Add some sage. If desired, you can brush the joints with olive oil and sprinkle some sage and seasoning on them. Then roast them in a preheated oven.

6   Add the rabbit joints to the tomato mixture, cover and cook on a very low flame for 90 minutes. If you see that the stew is drying up, then you have to add some more marinade. This dish can also be cooked as a casserole in a moderate oven. Garnish with olives.

7   You can serve this stew either with spaghetti and plenty of grated cheese or on its own with fresh, Maltese, crusty bread.

FRIED RABBIT WITH WINE AND GARLIC

FENEK MOQLI BL-INBID U TEWM

rabbit portions
red wine
olive oil
garlic cloves
fresh thyme
bay leaves
seasoning

1   Peel and chop the garlic cloves.

2   Place the rabbit portions in a large bowl and cover them with wine. Mix in the garlic, thyme, bay leaves and some seasoning. Leave some garlic for frying. Cover and leave in the fridge overnight.

3   Heat some oil in a large saucepan. Add the garlic and fry it for a few minutes. Don't fry until golden brown. Remove the rabbit pieces from the marinade and dry them with kitchen paper. Fry them until the rabbit meat is a deep, golden colour. Turn the rabbit portions occasionally during cooking and sprinkle some marinade over them.

4   Lower the flame, add some more marinade and cover the pan. Leave to simmer until the rabbit meat is tender. Check regularly to see that the mixture remains moist. Add more marinade if necessary.

BRAISED BEEF OLIVES

STUFFAT TAL-BRAGOLI TAC-CANGA

If you will be serving 2 beef olives per person, then the beef portions should consist of small sized cuts.

*4 thin slices of beef...
best cuts being rump or
top side*

*4 rashers of bacon, skin
removed*

1 hard boiled egg

chopped parsley

seasoning

For the sauce

*300ml gravy... use gravy
granules which you mix
with water*

300g chopped onions

200g peas

1 glass red wine

garlic

olive oil

sage

seasoning

1　Preheat the oven 180°C, gas mark 5.

2　If the beef slices are not thin enough, flatten them with a mallet. Season each slice. Put a bacon rasher in the centre of each slice together with one-fourth of a hard boiled egg. Sprinkle some chopped parsley on top.

3　Roll each slice from one end to the other, creating a small cylindrical shape. Use a couple of cocktail sticks (or some string ideal for cooking) to hold the olive in place so that it doesn't unroll.

4　Heat some oil in a medium sized pan and lightly fry the beef olives until they are cooked only from the outside. Remove the beef olives from the heat, but keep them warm.

5　Heat some oil in another saucepan and quickly fry the onions and garlic to a golden colour. Add the sage and cook for a further 3 minutes. Add the wine, gravy and peas. Bring the gravy to a boil.

6　Remove the beef olives from the pan and put them into a casserole. Add the gravy and season if necessary. Cover with a lid and continue cooking in the oven for about 80 minutes.

STUFFED BEEF FLANK

FALDA TAĊ-ĊANGA MIMLIJA

The flank is one of the cheapest cuts of beef, but it is ideal for use in a dish which needs long cooking time. The result will be a very tender and succulent dish. This dish can be prepared and cooked a day beforehand and warmed just before serving. When you buy the beef flank, ask the butcher to slit it open like a pocket.

1kg flank
2l water
300g minced beef
300g minced pork
80g grated cheese
2 eggs, lightly beaten
3 carrots, peeled and cut into cubes
2 marrows, cut into cubes
1 tbsp tomato paste
celery, chopped in small pieces
finely chopped parsley
seasoning

1   Put the minced meat in a large mixing bowl. Add the parsley, grated cheese and beaten eggs. Sprinkle some salt and freshly ground pepper. Mix well until all the ingredients are thoroughly combined.

2   Stuff the flank with this mixture and sew the ends closed with suitable thread.

3   Fill a large pan with water. Add the vegetables and bring them to a boil.

4   Lower the heat. Add the stuffed flank and continue cooking over very low heat for about 90 minutes. Check frequently to see whether you need to add more water. Should this be the case, always use hot water.

5   Remove the cooked flank from the broth. If desired, you can add some fine pasta and thus obtain a very nourishing soup.

6   Allow the flank to sit for about 15 minutes before slicing. Serve it either hot with potatoes, vegetables and gravy or cold with a crisp, green salad and sliced tomatoes.

TRIPE STEW

STUFFAT TAL-KIRXA

600g tripe
600g tomatoes
300g onions
200g peas
juice of 2 lemons, freshly squeezed
5 garlic cloves
1 glass white wine
oil
chilli pepper (optional)
seasoning

1   Wash the tripe and cut it in long pieces. Put the lemon juice and seasoning in a bowl and mix well. Marinate the tripe in this marinade for 30 minutes.

2   Peel the onions, garlic and tomatoes and chop them in medium sized pieces.

3   Heat some oil in a large saucepan and fry the onions and garlic to a golden colour.

4   Lower the heat. Add the tripe, chilli pepper (if using) and seasoning. Mix well and continue cooking.

5   Add the wine, peas and tomatoes and mix well. Check to see if the mix needs more seasoning. Continue cooking for a further hour, always on a very low flame.

6   Check frequently so that the stew doesn't dry up. Add some warm water in case this happens.

FRIED LIVER WITH GARLIC

FWIED MOQLI BIT-TEWM

800g liver

4 or 5 garlic cloves… use as much as desired

flour

parsley, finely chopped

mixed herbs

butter

seasoning

1   Clean the liver and slice it thinly.

2   Peel and finely chop the garlic.

3   Melt some butter in a large frying pan. Fry the garlic until it just turns to a golden brown colour.

4   Pass the liver through some seasoned flour. Shake off any excess.

5   Add the liver slices to the garlic and fry them on both sides. Don't overcook.

6   Place the cooked liver in a large serving dish with chopped parsley and mixed herbs sprinkled on top.

7   Serve with mashed potatoes.

GRILLED MALTESE SAUSAGES

ZALZETT MALTI MIXWI

Maltese sausages are a very special local delicacy. The main ingredients are pork mince, chopped parsley, chopped garlic and coriander with a substantial amount of sea salt.

Sausages are served in various ways. They can be boiled, added to *kawlata* (the Maltese vegetable soup with the addition of pork belly and Maltese sausage) or grilled. They can also be used as part of the filling used to stuff pork.

A more modern way of serving Maltese sausages is in slices on pizza or grilled.

Maltese sausages
½ glass white wine
mustard
freshly milled pepper

1   Preheat a non-stick frying pan.

2   Pour the wine in a bowl, add the mustard and some freshly milled pepper and mix well.

3   Spread this cream on the sausages.

4   Prick the sausages with a fork and grill them well. Turn them frequently while grilling so that they are well cooked all over.

MEATBALLS WITH TOMATO SAUCE

PULPETTI TAL-LAĦAM FIZ-ZALZA TAT-TADAM

600g minced beef... a combined mixture of minced beef and pork can be used instead

60g grated cheese

4 slices of bread

2 eggs, lightly beaten

tomato sauce

chopped parsley

chopped garlic

milk

seasoning

1   Preheat the oven 180°C, gas mark 4.

2   Put the minced meat in a large bowl.

3   Soak the bread in milk in another bowl. Drain well and add it to the meat. Mix well.

4   Add the chopped garlic, lightly beaten eggs, chopped parsley, grated cheese and seasoning. Mix well until all the ingredients blend together. It might be necessary to use your hands to mix the ingredients. Avoid using a food processor to blend the ingredients as over-processing can cause the mixture to become too soft and more pâté like.

5   Form the mixture into balls about the size of a large walnut. Don't flour your hands as this will just result in the meatball becoming stodgy. When forming the meatballs, try to compact them as much as possible by squeezing the mixture firmly before rolling them between the palms of your hands.

6   Place the meatballs in a baking dish. Don't put them too close to each other.

7   Add some water and cook in the preheated oven for 20 minutes until they begin to change colour.

8   In the meantime, prepare a plain tomato sauce in a large casserole.

9   Remove the meatballs from the oven, put them in the tomato sauce and cook for a further 40 minutes on low heat.

10   These meatballs can be either served as a meatball stew accompanied with some boiled or mashed potatoes or served on a bed of plain, boiled rice or pasta.

MEATLOAF

To ensure a perfect meatloaf, it is imperative that the meat should be very finely minced and well seasoned.

400g minced beef

400g minced pork

200g onions

60g grated cheese…
use best quality cheese
like Grana Padano or
Parmesan

4 slices of bread

3 eggs

garlic cloves

chopped parsley

fresh sage

milk

oil

seasoning

1   Heat the oven to 190°C, gas mark 5.

2   Place the minced meat in a large mixing bowl. Soak the bread in the milk, drain well and add it to the meat.

3   Lightly beat the eggs in a separate bowl and add them to the meat mixture. Add the grated cheese and mix well.

4   Peel and chop the onions and garlic. Heat some oil in a frying pan and quickly fry them, stirring frequently.

5   Add the fried onions and garlic to the meat mixture. Add the chopped parsley and some chopped, fresh sage. Mix well. Check to see whether the mixture needs more seasoning. Mix until all the ingredients are blended together.

6   Line a loaf tin with stretch and seal, allowing some to hang over the tin's edges.

7   Fill the loaf tin with the meat mixture. Flatten the top and cover it with stretch and seal. Cover with aluminium foil.

8   Put the loaf tin into a baking dish. Pour hot water from the kettle into the baking dish to come halfway up the loaf tin. Bake for 1 hour until the loaf shrinks from the tin's sides.

9   This method of cooking is known as *bain marie*. Baking the loaf this way ensures that it cooks through evenly and stays moist.

10   Cool the meatloaf in the tin for 10 minutes, drain off any excess liquid and turn it out onto a serving plate. Cut it into thick slices and serve warm or cold with salad.

FISH

STUFFED CALAMARI

KLAMARI MIMLIJIN

4 medium sized calamari
150g onions
150g mushrooms
60g tomatoes
30g black olives
garlic
fresh mint
olive oil
seasoning

Clean the calamari if not purchased already so.

Holding the body firmly, grasp the head and pull gently, twisting if necessary, to pull the head away from the body without breaking the ink sac. The internal body and tentacles will come out with it.

Cut the tentacles from the head just below the eyes and set aside. At the centre of the tentacles is a small beak. Squeeze to remove it and discard.

At the top of the body, there is a clear piece of cartilage. Pull it out and discard as well.

If the calamari has an outer, spotted, membrane-type skin, pull it off and discard too.

Wash the tube carefully, inside and out, together with the tentacles under cold running water. Set all the cleaned calamari aside to drain.

Finely chop the tentacles and set them aside. Pit the olives, slice them into thin slivers and set them aside.

Peel and finely chop the onions and garlic. Wash and finely chop as well the mushrooms, tomatoes and mint leaves.

Heat some olive oil in a large frying pan, add the onions and garlic and fry them gently until soft and golden. Add all of the remaining chopped ingredients and continue cooking for a few more minutes, stirring continually.

Preheat the oven 180°C, gas mark 3.

Add the chopped tentacles and fry for a further 5 minutes, stirring often.

Stuff the calamari with the mixture, allowing a little room for the stuffing to expand during cooking. Seal the ends with cocktail sticks.

Lightly grease a baking dish with olive oil and place the stuffed calamari in it.

Cook in the oven for about 45 minutes.

Serve hot with tomato sauce.

STUFFED PILOT FISH

FANFRI MIMLIJIN

4 medium sized pilot fish
150g fresh, white
breadcrumbs
50g onions, chopped
fresh mint, finely chopped
lemon zest and juice
olive oil and vinegar
seasoning

Thoroughly clean the fish and pat them dry with kitchen paper.

Mix together the onions, breadcrumbs, lemon zest, mint, oil and vinegar in a large bowl. Sprinkle some seasoning and mix again.

Preheat the oven 170°C, gas mark 3.

Using a sharp knife, make an incision in the middle of each fish and cut under the top fillet to make a pocket. Season the inside with salt and freshly ground black pepper. Pack the breadcrumb mixture into the pocket, then fold the pocket back over to enclose the stuffing.

Place the fish in an ovenproof dish lined with well greased aluminium foil.

Transfer to the oven and bake for 40 minutes or until cooked through.

SWORDFISH MDINA

PIXXISPAD MDINA

4 swordfish steak
200g onions
200g tomatoes
200g mushrooms
3 or 4 garlic heads
fresh mint or basil
freshly squeezed lemon juice
grated lemon rind
olive oil
seasoning

Marinate the swordfish steak for 30 minutes.

Preheat the grill and, once hot, grill the swordfish steak on both sides. There is no need for it to be thoroughly cooked.

Peel and finely chop the onions and garlic.

Heat some olive oil in a frying pan and quickly fry the onions and garlic.

Wash and chop the tomatoes and mushrooms in medium sized pieces. Add them to the onion mixture. Continue cooking for a few minutes, stirring frequently.

Add the lemon zest and juice as well as the fresh herbs.

Lower the heat, add the swordfish steak and continue cooking for about 15 more minutes.

WHITEBAIT PATTIES

PULPETTI TAL-MAKKU

½kg whitebait

1 egg yolk

flour or semolina

garlic cloves

fresh parsley, finely chopped

coriander, crushed a bit

frying oil

seasoning

Roughly cut the fish. Peel and crush the garlic.

Mix well together the egg yolk, crushed garlic, coriander and chopped parsley in a bowl. Add some flour, seasoning and the whitebait to this mixture. Mix until all the ingredients are well combined.

Using your hands, shape the mixture into small, round patties.

Put some semolina on a large, flat plate and pass these patties in it.

Heat a frying pan on medium-high heat, and once heated, add the oil.

Gently drop the raw patties into the hot oil. Fry the patties until they are a deep golden colour, turning them to ensure that each side is done.

Keep them in a warm place until they are ready to be served.

Serve hot with lemon wedges, tartar sauce and a crisp, green salad.

TUNA CASSEROLE

CASSEROLE TAT-TONN

Casseroles are complete meals served out of just one dish. In addition, most casseroles freeze well; hence, cooks can make multiple casseroles ahead of time and just pop them in the oven for a dinner on a busy day. An added advantage is that a casserole will often take care of itself, especially when cooked or finished off in an oven. It's important to envelope all ingredients in water to allow the dish to gently simmer away.

600g tuna
600g potatoes
200g onions
200g tomatoes
200g leeks
2 glasses water
garlic cloves
olive oil
freshly squeezed lemon juice and zest
finely chopped parsley

1   Wash the tuna well and remove all skin and bones. Cut into 4 portions. Place the tuna portions in a shallow dish and pour the fresh lemon juice over them. Cover and put them in the fridge.

2   Preheat the oven 170°C, gas mark 3.

3   Peel and thinly slice the potatoes and onions. Wash and thinly slice the tomatoes. Peel and chop the leeks and garlic.

4   Place one layer of potatoes, onions and tomatoes on the bottom of a lightly greased casserole dish. Remove the tuna portions from the lemon juice and place them on the vegetable mixture. Put a layer of chopped leeks and garlic on them. Season and sprinkle some lemon zest on top.

5   Cover with the remaining potatoes and onions. Season and add olive oil and water.

6   Put on the lid and cook for 70 minutes. Remove the lid and cook for a further 20 minutes.

7   Before serving, sprinkle some chopped parsley on top.

OCTOPUS STEW

STUFFAT TAL-QARNIT

For a really tender octopus, ask your fishmonger to prepare the octopus in a way that it's ready for cooking. Once home, place it in the freezer for at least 3 weeks before cooking.

800g octopus

600ml red wine

200g potatoes, peeled and cut into medium sized chunks

150g tomatoes, peeled and chopped

100g onions, peeled and finely chopped

100g black olives, pitted and chopped

100g peas

50g tomato paste

4 garlic cloves, peeled and crushed

lemon zest

capers

marjoram and basil

seasoning

olive oil

Defrost the octopus and rinse it thoroughly, then chop it into bite-sized pieces. Fill a saucepan with water and bring it to a boil. Cook the octopus for about 20 minutes.

Heat some olive oil in a large frying pan and quickly fry the onions and garlic until golden. Lower the heat and add the tomatoes, olives, capers, tomato paste and lemon zest. Mix well. Add some water and leave to simmer for about 10 minutes.

Remove the octopus pieces from water and add them to the tomato mixture. Add the marjoram and basil and half of the wine. Cover the pan and leave to simmer over low heat for at least 1 hour.

Add the potatoes, peas and the rest of the wine. Continue cooking, always on low heat, for another ½ hour.

Check the octopus for tenderness and keep on cooking until it is done. Take care that the stew doesn't boil dry. Add some hot water should this be the case.

Check for seasoning before serving. Serve with fresh, Maltese, crusty bread.

BOILED OCTOPUS SALAD

INSALATA TAL-QARNIT MGĦOLLI

800g octopus
1 lemon, cut into wedges
lemon zest
black olives, pitted
capers
fresh parsley, finely chopped
fresh marjoram
fresh mint
extra virgin olive oil

Defrost the octopus and cut it into large chunks.

Fill a large pot with water. Bring it to a boil and add the octopus chunks. Reduce the heat to a simmer. Continue to cook until the octopus chunks are fork tender, i.e., about 25 to 30 minutes.

Strain the octopus chunks and place them in a large salad bowl.

Add the black olives, capers, lemon zest and fresh herbs. Drizzle over some olive oil.

Decorate with the lemon wedges and sprinkle the finely chopped parsley over them.

Serve with warm Maltese ftira or crusty bread.

FRIED LAMPUKI

LAMPUKI MOQLIJIN

800g lampuki
flour
fresh lemon wedges
olive oil
seasoning

Carefully clean the fish and cut off the head and tail. Cut it into 4 portions.

Season some flour and pass the fish through it. Shake off any excess.

Heat some olive oil in a large frying pan. Fry the fish on very low heat until golden brown in colour.

Serve with fresh lemon wedges, chips and a green salad.

SALT COD STEW

STUFFAT TAL-BAKKALJAW

600g salt cod
600g potatoes
300g pumpkin
1 medium cauliflower
2 onions
2 garlic cloves
80g peas
8 black olives, destoned and chopped
2 tbsp olive oil
2 tbsp tomato paste
1 tbsp fresh mint
½ tbsp ground chilli pepper (optional)
lemon slices
oil

Rinse any excess salt off the cod. Place the cod pieces into a large bowl and cover them with cold water and some lemon slices. Leave them to soak in the fridge for at least 24 hours, changing the water three to four times. Alternatively, soak for 3 days for best results; cooked cod will be more fleshy and tender. Drain them well and flake them into large pieces, discarding the skin and any bones.

Peel and chop the onions and garlic.

Remove the pumpkin rind and cut it into cubes. Wash the cauliflower and separate the florets. Peel, wash and cut the potatoes into quarters. Place all the vegetables in a bowl.

Heat some oil in a large saucepan and fry the chopped onions and garlic. Stir frequently. The onions should be just lightly brown.

Add the vegetables, cod, olives, tomato paste, herbs and enough water to cover.

Cover with a lid and cook on a moderate flame until the stew comes to a boil.

Lower the heat and continue simmering until you obtain a thick and juicy stew.

SALT COD SALAD

INSALATA TAL-BAKKALJAW

The balance of salt cod, potatoes, onions and fresh parsley makes this salad extremely tasty.

500g salt cod

400g potatoes

50g pickled onions

50g black olives, destoned and chopped

4 garlic cloves, peeled and finely chopped

2 or 3 leeks

2 hard boiled eggs

2 tbsp balsamic vinegar

1 large tomato, thinly sliced

1 small bunch of fresh parsley

bay leaf

lemon slices

freshly ground black pepper

Rinse any excess salt off the cod. Place the cod into a large bowl and cover it with cold water. Leave it to soak in the fridge for at least 24 hours, changing the water three to four times. If upon tasting a small piece after allotted time has lapsed the cod is still salty, soak it for a bit longer.

Put the cod into a pan with the bay leaf and cover it with fresh, cold water. Bring it to just below boiling point over medium heat. Remove the pan from the heat and leave it to stand for about 10 minutes.

Remove the cod from the water and leave it to cool, setting the water aside. Once cooled, remove the cod's skin and any bones and flake the flesh with a fork. Place it in a large bowl.

Peel and quarter the potatoes and cook them, over medium-high heat in the poaching water previously put aside, for about 15 minutes or until tender. Don't overcook them. Drain, allow to cool slightly and then add them to the cod.

Wash, peel and finely chop the leeks. Add them to the cod and potatoes. Add the sliced tomato and mix gently together.

Wash and trim the parsley, discarding the stems. Dry and finely chop the leaves. Add the chopped parsley leaves to the potatoes and cod.

Combine the oil, vinegar, garlic and pepper in a bowl. Whisk the vinaigrette until the ingredients are thoroughly blended. Toss the salad with the vinaigrette until all the ingredients are coated.

Transfer the salad to a platter and garnish the edges with olives, wedges of hard boiled egg and pickled onions cut in slices.

Serve at room temperature or refrigerate until serving.

SALT COD FRITTERS

SFINEĠ TAL-BAKKALJAW

This Maltese delicacy was once sold by street hawkers, especially in villages. These small pastries similar to ravioli are filled with small pieces of cod and deep fried. They must be eaten hot.

400g salt cod

150g plain flour

2 tomatoes, peeled and chopped

2 garlic cloves, peeled and chopped

1 tsp baking powder

freshly squeezed lemon juice

bay leaf

frying oil

Rinse any excess salt off the cod. Place the cod into a large bowl and cover it with cold water. Leave it to soak in the fridge for at least 24 hours, changing the water three to four times. If upon tasting a small piece after allotted time has lapsed the cod is still salty, soak it for a bit longer.

Put the cod into a pan with the bay leaf and cover it with fresh, cold water. Bring it to just below boiling point over medium heat. Remove the pan from the heat and leave it to stand for about 10 minutes.

Remove the cod from the water and leave it to cool, setting the water aside. Once cooled, remove the cod's skin and any bones and flake the flesh with a fork. Place it in a large bowl. Add the tomatoes and chopped garlic. Mix well.

Meanwhile, prepare the batter. Sift the flour together with the baking powder in a bowl. Add some lemon juice and enough water to form a thick batter; thick enough to be able to cover the cod completely. Allow it to rest for a couple of hours.

Add the cod mixture to the batter and mix well.

Heat some deep frying oil in a large saucepan.

Form the cod mixture into approximately 20 small balls using a spoon and fry in batches, about 5-6 at a time, for 3 minutes or until a deep golden brown.

Drain the cod fritters on kitchen paper and serve piping hot.

ANCHOVY PUFFS

SFINEĠ TAL-INĊOVA

150g plain flour
100g anchovy fillets
1tsp baking powder
deep frying oil

Soak the anchovies for about an hour in cold milk or water to remove some of the salt.

Meanwhile, prepare the batter same as for the salt cod fritters, but omitting the lemon juice (see page 130).

Remove the anchovies from the milk and pat them dry with kitchen paper. Peel off the fillet from one side and then remove the backbone and tail from the other fillet.

Heat some deep frying oil in a large saucepan.

Dip each anchovy fillet in the batter and fry until golden.

Drain the anchovy fillets on kitchen paper and serve piping hot.

FRIED LAMPUKI WITH TOMATO SAUCE

LAMPUKI MOQLIJIN BIZ-ZALZA TAT-TADAM

4 lampuki fillets
600g tomatoes
50g capers
3 or 4 garlic cloves
flour
fresh basil
fresh lemon wedges
olive oil
seasoning

Peel and finely chop the garlic. Peel and cut the tomatoes in medium sized pieces. Put them in separate bowls.

Heat some olive oil in a large frying pan and quickly fry the chopped garlic. Stir frequently so that the garlic doesn't brown. Add the tomatoes and fresh basil. Mash and squash the tomatoes as much as you can using the back of a wooden spoon. Cook on a moderately low flame for about 20 minutes. Check for seasoning and add the capers. Remove from over the heat.

Preheat the oven 180°C, gas mark 4.

Season some flour and pass the lampuki fillets through it. Shake off any excess. Heat some olive oil in a different sauté pan. Cook the floured fillets on a moderate flame until golden brown in colour.

Put the lampuki fillets in an oven dish and pour the sauce over them. Cook in the oven for 10 minutes.

Serve with fresh lemon wedges and fresh basil leaves or a parsley sprig.

LAMPUKI LA VALLETTE

LAMPUKI LA VALLETTE

4 lampuki fillets
2 large potatoes
60g Gouda cheese
finely chopped parsley
freshly grated lemon rind
fresh lemon wedges
olive oil
fennel seeds
seasoning

1   Preheat the oven 180°C, gas mark 4.

2   Peel and grate the potatoes. Place them into a large bowl and add the grated cheese and lemon rind. Mix well until well combined, then season with salt and freshly ground black pepper.

3   Add the chopped parsley and some fennel seeds and mix.

4   Lightly grease a baking tray or line it with a baking sheet. Lay the l*ampuki* fillets on the baking sheet. Cover them with the potato mixture. Season, pour some olive oil and bake in the medium to hot oven for about 35 minutes or until lightly browned.

5   Serve with fresh lemon wedges.

LAMPUKI WITH PICKLED ONIONS

LAMPUKI BIL-BASAL TAL-PIKLES

1kg lampuki
½kg tomatoes, peeled and chopped
300g pickled onions
25g tomato paste
garlic cloves, peeled and chopped
flour
olive oil
mint
seasoning

Clean the fish. Remove the head and tail and cut it into pieces about 8cm long.

Heat some olive oil in a large, deep frying pan. Pass the fish pieces through the flour and fry them until golden. Remove the fish pieces and put them aside to cool.

Add some more olive oil and fry the garlic. Add the tomatoes, tomato paste and mint. Check for seasoning. Lower the heat and simmer for about 15 minutes.

Meanwhile, remove all the bones from the cooled fish pieces. Slice the onions.

Add half of the onions to the sauce and mix well.

Place the fish pieces in a large serving dish. Pour the onion and tomato sauce over them.

Garnish with the remainder of the pickled onions.

BAKED LAMPUKI

LAMPUKI FIL-FORN BIL-PATATA

4 medium sized lampuki
¾kg potatoes
50g onions
garlic cloves
marjoram
fennel seeds
oil
seasoning

Clean the fish.

Preheat the oven 180°C, gas mark 4.

Peel the potatoes and onions and cut them into thick slices. Peel and chop the garlic in medium sized pieces.

Pour a little oil in a baking dish. Put a layer of potatoes and onions and sprinkle some garlic.

Lay the fish on the potatoes and onions. Sprinkle some marjoram and garlic and season well.

Cover the fish with the remaining potatoes, onions and garlic. Sprinkle some fennel seeds and seasoning.

Pour some more oil and water and bake for at least 90 minutes.

Serve with a crisp, green salad.

LAMPUKI WITH CAPER SAUCE

LAMPUKI BIZ-ZALZA TAL-KAPPAR

1kg lampuki
500g tomatoes
200g onions
150g capers
garlic cloves
flour
olive oil
fresh lemon zest
mint
seasoning

1. Peel and chop the tomatoes, onions and garlic. Put them in separate bowls.

2. Clean the fish. Remove the head and tail and cut it into pieces about 8cm long.

3. Heat some olive oil in a large saucepan. Pass the fish pieces through the flour and fry them until they obtain a golden colour.

4. Heat some olive oil in another frying pan and quickly fry the onions and garlic until they obtain a light golden colour.

5. Lower the heat, add the tomatoes and tomato paste and simmer for about 10 minutes. Add the capers, lemon zest and mint. Check for seasoning and continue simmering for a further 10 minutes.

6. Add the fish pieces to the sauce and continue cooking for a further 5 minutes.

7. Serve hot.

VEGETABLES

STUFFED AUBERGINES

BRUNĠIEL MIMLI

2 medium sized aubergines

400g minced meat... use either only pork or beef or a mixture of both

75g chopped onions

50g tomato paste

25g grated Parmesan cheese

2 eggs

oil

salt and freshly ground pepper

1   Wash and cut the aubergines in half (lengthwise) and boil them for 6 minutes.

2   Scoop the pulp from inside with a teaspoon, chop and put it in a bowl.

3   Heat some oil in a frying pan and lightly fry the onions. Add the minced meat and chopped aubergine filling. Cook for 10 minutes, stirring frequently.

4   Add the tomato paste, salt and pepper. Remove the pan from over the heat and leave the mixture to cool.

5   Preheat the oven 180°C, gas mark 4.

6   Add the eggs and cheese to the mixture and mix well.

7   Stuff the aubergines with this mixture.

8   Put the aubergines in a baking dish and bake in the preheated oven for 35 to 40 minutes.

AUBERGINE AND GREEN PEPPERS IN PIQUANT SAUCE

BRUNĠIEL U BŻAR AĦDAR F'ZALZA PIKKANTI

1 large aubergine
200g green peppers
200g chopped tomatoes
150g onions
25g tomato paste
garlic clove
olive oil
water
salt and freshly ground pepper

1   Wash, peel and slice the aubergine into medium sized slices.

2   Wash and cut the green peppers into six portions and remove the seeds.

3   Peel and chop finely the onions and garlic.

4   Heat some olive oil in a large frying pan and fry the onions and garlic. Add the sliced aubergine and peppers. Cook on low heat for 10 minutes.

5   Peel and chop the tomatoes in quarters and add them to the aubergine mixture. Add the tomato paste and water. Cook for 15 minutes, stirring frequently.

6   Season.

This tangy dish can be served either hot or cold.

GREEN PEPPERS STUFFED WITH LAMPUKI

BŻAR AĦDAR MIMLI BIL-LAMPUKI

300g cooked lampuki
150g cooked rice
50g onions
25g tomato paste
25g chopped olives
4 large green peppers
2 lightly beaten eggs
finely chopped parsley
a mixture of finely chopped basil and mint leaves
oil
water
salt and freshly ground pepper

1   Cut the top of each pepper and remove the seeds. Wash the deseeded peppers and leave them to drain. Keep the pepper tops.

2   Peel and chop the onions.

3   Heat some oil in a large frying pan and fry the onions until they become golden brown. Add the tomato paste and water and simmer for 10 minutes.

4   Add the cooked rice, olives, parsley, seasoning, herbs and the flaked *lampuki*. Pay special attention to remove all fish bones. Finally, add the eggs. Continue simmering for a further 10 minutes, stirring frequently.

5   Preheat the oven 180°C, gas mark 4.

6   Fill the green peppers with this mixture and place the tops back in their place. Put the peppers in a baking dish.

7   Bake in the moderately heated oven for about 60 to 75 minutes.

 This dish can be served either hot or cold.

STUFFED GLOBE ARTICHOKES

QAQOĊĊ MIMLI BL-INĊOVA

4 globe artichokes
150g fresh breadcrumbs
75g anchovy fillets
50g olives
crushed garlic
parsley
oil and vinegar
salt and freshly ground pepper

1   Chop the anchovy fillets, garlic, olives and parsley and put them in a mixing bowl. Add the breadcrumbs and mix well.

2   Add the oil and vinegar and work into a dry paste. Season according to taste.

3   Wash the artichokes and fill between the leaves with this mixture.

4   Place the artichokes upright in a small saucepan. Half cover them with water and add some oil. Cover them with a lid, bring them to a boil and simmer for 1 hour.

5   Serve hot.

BROAD BEANS WITH GARLIC

FUL BIT-TEWM

2kg broad beans
600ml water
3-4 garlic cloves
finely chopped parsley
olive oil
vinegar
salt and freshly ground pepper

1   Skin the beans.

2   Place them into a small pan. Add the garlic and plenty of water. Bring to a boil.

3   Add all the other ingredients. Simmer until the beans are tender.

4   Serve hot.

STUFFED POTATOES

PATATA MIMLIJA

4 large potatoes

200g minced meat... use either beef or pork or a mixture of both

75g chopped onions

25g grated cheese

25g tomato paste

2 lightly beaten eggs

oil

salt and freshly ground pepper

1   Peel the potatoes. Remove the top and scoop out some of the inside. Take care so as not to break the sides of the potatoes.

2   Peel and chop the onions.

3   Heat some oil in a frying pan and quickly fry the onions. Stir all the time to make sure that they don't brown.

4   Add the minced meat and cook until it is almost done. Add the tomato paste and some water. Simmer for about 5 minutes.

5   Add the cheese and eggs and continue to cook. Stir all the time until the mixture is thick. Season.

6   Preheat the oven 180°C, gas mark 4.

7   Stuff the potatoes with this mixture and sprinkle some cheese on top.

8   Bake in the oven for 1½ to 2 hours.

MARROWS STUFFED WITH RICOTTA

QARABAGĦLI MIMLI BL-IRKOTTA

4 medium sized marrows
200g ricotta
50g grated cheese
2 eggs
finely chopped parsley
semolina
salt and freshly ground pepper

1   Wash the marrows. Remove the tops and carefully scoop the insides, taking care not to break them.

2   Put the ricotta into a large mixing bowl and beat it well until it obtains a creamy texture. Add the eggs, parsley and cheese. Season with salt and pepper and mix everything well.

3   Fill the marrows with this mixture.

4   Put some semolina on a flat plate and dip the top of the marrows into it.

5   Place the stuffed marrows into a small pan or casserole and half cover them with water. Bring them to a boil and simmer until cooked. Check frequently to make sure that there is always enough water in the pan.

STUFFED LONG MARROWS

QARA' TWIL MIMLI BIL-LAHAM

1kg long marrows

1kg potatoes

1kg onions

600g minced meat… use either pork or beef or veal or a mixture of all three

50g grated cheese

25g tomato paste

garlic clove

finely chopped parsley

olive oil

salt and freshly ground pepper

1   Peel and cut the marrows into pieces about 10cm long.

2   Scoop out the insides.

3   Continue cooking following the same method as for 'Marrows Stuffed with Meat' (see page 156).

MARROWS STUFFED WITH MEAT

QARABAGĦLI MIMLI BIL-LAĦAM

4 large marrows
1kg potatoes
600g minced meat... use either pork or beef or veal or a mixture of all three
100g onions
50g grated cheese
25g tomato paste
2 eggs
garlic clove
finely chopped parsley
olive oil
salt and freshly ground pepper

1   Wash and cut the tops of the marrows and scoop out the insides. Chop the pulp and put it in a bowl.

2   Peel and chop the onions and garlic.

3   Heat some olive oil in a large frying pan and quickly fry the onions and garlic, taking care not to brown them. Stir frequently.

4   Lower the heat and add the tomato paste and meat. Stir and continue cooking for about 15-20 minutes or until the minced meat is cooked.

5   Add the chopped marrow pulp and cook for a few more minutes. Remove from over the heat and allow to cool.

6   Preheat the oven 180°C, gas mark 4.

7   Add the eggs, cheese, parsley and seasoning. Mix well.

8   Fill the marrows with this mixture and place them on a bed of peeled and sliced potatoes.

9   Bake in the preheated oven for 1 to 1½ hours.

CREAMED SPINACH WITH EGG

SPINAĊI BIL-BAJD U KREMA FRISKA

This is a very quick snack my grandma used to make for us when we were children.

fresh spinach
fresh cream
fresh nutmeg
1 egg
a knob of butter
oil
seasoning

1   Remove the stalk from the spinach. Wash and cook the spinach without adding any water. Don't overcook since it will lose its bright, green colour.

2   Remove the cooked spinach from the pan, drain it well and put it in a large mixing bowl. Add some freshly grated nutmeg and seasoning.

3   Heat some oil in a large frying pan and cook the spinach over low heat until all the liquid is absorbed. Stir the spinach frequently while cooking. Add 2 tablespoons of fresh cream. Mix well.

4   Melt the butter in another frying pan and fry the egg. Season according to taste.

5   Serve the egg on top of the spinach with potatoes.

DRIED BEAN PÂTÉ

BIGILLA

Bigilla is a traditional Maltese snack made out of a special type of bean. Used beans are similar to broad beans, but are much smaller, with a darker and harder skin. They are locally called *ful ta' Ġirba* (Djerba beans). Up to a few years ago, *bigilla* was sold by street vendors in villages in Malta and Gozo. Nowadays, it can be bought from the delicatessen counter of supermarkets. It is served either with Maltese g*alletti* or crusty bread.

400g dried broad beans
3-4 garlic cloves
finely chopped parsley
chilli pepper
olive oil
vinegar
bicarbonate of soda

1   Soak the beans in salted water with some bicarbonate of soda for 24 hours.

2   Rinse the beans well, put them in a pan and cook them in plenty of salted water. Bring them to a boil and simmer until they are cooked. Don't leave the beans short of water as they may stick to the pan's bottom and burn.

3   Mince the beans and season them. Add some olive oil and place the mixture into a serving dish.

4   Chop the parsley. Peel and crush the garlic and chilli pepper. Mix them with some oil and vinegar. Pour this sauce over the beans.

PIES & TARTS

RABBIT PIE

TORTA TAL-FENEK

600g shortcrust pastry
1kg rabbit meat
200g tomatoes
200g onions
200g potatoes
150g peas
150g carrots
30g tomato paste
olive oil
garlic
thyme
bay leaves
seasoning

1   Prepare the pastry.

2   Wash the tomatoes and carrots and chop them in medium sized pieces. Peel the potatoes, garlic and onions and chop them in small pieces. Cut the rabbit meat in cubes.

3   Preheat the oven 180°C, gas mark 4.

4   Heat some olive oil in a large frying pan and fry the chopped onions and garlic until they are golden brown. Add the rabbit meat. Stir in some thyme and bay leaves and fry for a few minutes. Add the carrots and potatoes. Mix well and cook for a further 10 minutes.

5   Add the tomatoes and peas. Remove the bay leaves and check the mixture to see if it needs seasoning.

6   Roll out half the pastry and line a lightly greased and floured 25cm tin with it. Fill it with the mixture.

7   Brush the edges with water and cover the pie with the remaining pastry. Make a few slits in the top of the pastry to let out the steam and prevent the crust from going soggy.

8   Brush the top with a lightly beaten egg and sprinkle some sesame seeds if desired.

9   Bake in the hot oven for 45-55 minutes or until the pastry turns golden.

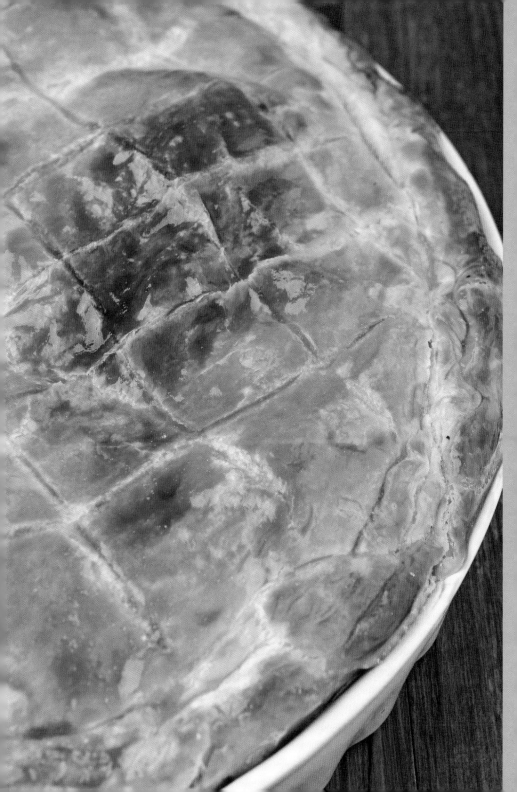

LAMPUKI PIE

TORTA TAL-LAMPUKI

600g shortcrust pastry

750g lampuki

250g tomatoes, peeled and chopped

250g cauliflower, boiled

250g tomato purée

250g onions, chopped

200g spinach, cooked

150g peas

100g black olives, destoned and chopped

3-4 garlic cloves, chopped

2 eggs

1 egg, lightly beaten

olive oil

lemon zest

fresh mint

fresh marjoram

seasoning

sesame seeds

1   Prepare the pastry.

2   Clean the fish and either steam or boil it. Remove all bones when it cools.

3   Preheat the oven 190°C, gas mark 5.

4   Fry the onions and garlic in olive oil until they are soft and golden. Lower the heat and add the fish, spinach, peas, chopped cauliflower, olives, tomatoes, tomato purée, lemon zest, mint, marjoram and seasoning. Mix well. Cook for a few minutes. Remove from over the heat and add the lightly beaten eggs when slightly cool. Mix well.

5   Roll out half the pastry and line a lightly greased and floured pie dish it. Fill it with the *lampuki* mixture.

6   Brush the edges with water. Use the rest of the pastry to cover the pie and seal the edges by pressing them well together. Make a few slits in the top of the pie. If you have some pastry left over, you can form it into shapes and decorate the top of the pie with them.

7   Brush with the lightly beaten egg and sprinkle some sesame seeds if desired.

8   Bake for about 50 minutes or until the pastry is crisp and golden.

RICOTTA PIE

TORTA TAL-IRKOTTA

600g shortcrust pastry
1kg ricotta
100g grated cheese
4 soft cheeselets
4 eggs
1 lightly beaten egg
finely chopped parsley
freshly grated nutmeg
seasoning
sesame seeds

1 Prepare the pastry.

2 Preheat the oven 180°C, gas mark 4.

3 Put the ricotta in a large bowl and mash it either with a fork or a potato masher. Mash until the ricotta is smooth and creamy.

4 Add the chopped parsley and eggs to the ricotta mixture and blend well. Add seasoning and freshly grated nutmeg. Mix the ingredients well together.

5 Roll out half the pastry on a lightly floured table and line a lightly greased 25 or 30cm pie dish with it. Fill the dish with the ricotta mixture.

6 Roll out the remaining pastry. Moisten the edges of the pie dish and cover the pie dish with it.

7 Seal the rim of the pastry to the dish by pressing the back of a fork down onto the pastry all the way around the edge. Cut two slits in the top of the pastry lid to allow the steam to escape.

8 Brush with the lightly beaten egg and sprinkle some sesame seeds if desired.

9 Bake for about 50-55 minutes or until the pastry turns golden brown in colour.

SPINACH AND TUNA PIE

TORTA TAL-ISPINAĊI U TONN TAŻ-ŻEJT

800g shortcrust pastry
1 kg cooked spinach
200g leeks
100g black olives,
destoned and chopped
3 or 4 garlic cloves
1 large tin of tuna in brine
1 egg, lightly beaten
fresh basil, chopped
freshly grated nutmeg
grated lemon rind
olive oil
sesame seeds
seasoning

1   Prepare the pastry.

2   Wash, peel and chop the leeks. Peel and chop the garlic.

3   Heat some oil in a large frying pan and fry the leeks and onions to a nice, golden colour.

4   Add the chopped spinach, drained tuna, freshly grated nutmeg, chopped basil, chopped olives, grated lemon rind and seasoning.

5   Mix carefully so as not to squash the mixture.

6   Preheat the oven 180°C, gas mark 4.

7   Roll out half the pastry on a lightly floured table and line a pie dish with it. Fill it with the tuna mixture.

8   Roll out the remaining pastry. Moisten the edges of the pie dish and cover the pie dish with it.

9   Seal the rim of the pastry to the dish by pressing the back of a fork down onto the pastry all the way around the edge; a decorative pattern in itself.

10   Cut two slits in the top of the pastry lid to allow the steam to escape.

11   Cut out several shapes from the remaining pastry using a sharp knife and position them on top of the pastry cover.

12   Brush the beaten egg over the pastry cover. Sprinkle some sesame seeds if desired.

13   Bake for 60 minutes or until the pastry turns golden brown in colour.

PUMPKIN PIE

TORTA TAL-QARGĦA ĦAMRA

This pie is a typical Maltese dish and is very popular in the north of Malta and in Gozo. Capers are often substituted with sultanas in some households.

600g shortcrust pastry

500g pumpkin, peeled, deseeded and diced

300g long grain rice

300g onions, peeled and finely chopped

150g black olives, destoned and cut in large pieces

100g anchovy fillets

2 large tins of tuna fish in oil

4 garlic cloves, peeled and finely chopped

3 tbsp capers

1 egg, lightly beaten

fresh marjoram

fresh mint

sesame seeds

oil

seasoning

1   Prepare the pastry. Lightly grease a 24cm diameter pie dish and line it with damp baking paper.

2   Boil the rice in abundant salted water for half the time stipulated on the packet, then drain immediately and put it aside to cool.

3   Heat some oil in a large deep frying pan. Quickly fry the onions and garlic until they are soft and golden.

4   Lower the heat. Add the pumpkin and continue cooking for a few more minutes.

5   Add the olives and capers and continue cooking until all the ingredients are soft. Stir frequently. If the mixture starts to stick to the pan's bottom, either add some white wine or some water.

6   Add the tuna, anchovies, herbs and cooked rice to the cooked mixture. Stir the mixture and season it with salt and pepper. Leave it to cool.

7   Preheat the oven 190°C, gas mark 5.

8   Divide the pastry in 2. One piece should be a little smaller than the other.

9   Roll out the larger piece of pastry on a lightly floured table top and line the pie dish with it.

10 Fill it with the pumpkin mixture and press it down lightly. Moisten the outside edges of the pastry with a little water.

11 Roll out the other piece of pastry and use it to make a lid for the pie. Using the prongs of a fork, press down onto the moistened edges of the pastry.

12 Make a few slits in the top of the pie. Brush the pastry lid with the beaten egg. Sprinkle some sesame seeds if desired.

13 Bake the pie for around 45 minutes or until the pastry turns golden.

SNACKS

FTIRA

Every country has its own distinctive bread in shape and form. But the bread that can be found in Mediterranean countries is something exceptional. Even tiny Malta can boast of its typical bread.

Here we have our much loved *ftira*. It is a semi flat bread in the shape of a disc. It resembles a *ciabatta*, but it has the shape of a large ring. The texture is superb. You simply have to taste it to be able to appreciate it!

It is very popular during the summer months, when you can split it, spread it with tomato paste and literally drench it with olive oil. You can then add anything you fancy: tinned tuna, olives, rocket leaves, anchovies, fresh basil and a generous sprinkling of salt and pepper. Instead of tomato paste you can rub fresh tomatoes. The result is a heavenly meal fit for a king!

You can also spread it with butter and some mustard. Then fill it with fresh smoked ham or salami, cheese, sliced hard boiled eggs and sliced tomatoes. Any way you fill it, it is simply not for dieters!

Nowadays, you will find it listed on each and every existent menu; from that of the most humble coffee shop in every village to that of the most chic and modern coffee shop in different towns.

If you happen to be in Malta during the summer months and go to the beach, you will realise that the majority of the people are all eating *ftira*.

If you want a different taste of the *ftira*, then all you have to do is to try out one of the following recipes. You buy the dough from the baker, fill it and then bake it. Remember to buy bread dough and not pizza dough. The smell of the *ftira* being baked is something divine! Nothing beats the taste of something home baked. The end result is a mix of pizza, *ftira* and *ciabatta*, but with the matchless taste of something typically Maltese!

FTIRA WITH PORK AND RICOTTA

FTIRA BIL-MAJJAL U RKOTTA

400g bread dough (not pizza dough)

300g ricotta

200g pork belly

200g onions, chopped

200g fresh broad beans, skinned

freshly grated nutmeg

olive oil

sesame seeds (optional)

seasoning

1   Put the ricotta in a large bowl and mash it with a fork. Add the seasoning and some freshly grated nutmeg. Add half of the broad beans and mix well.

2   Peel and chop the onions in small pieces. Clean the pork belly and cut it into small cubes.

3   Preheat the oven 190°C, gas mark 5.

4   Heat some olive oil in a pan and lightly fry the onions for a few minutes. Add the pork belly and continue cooking for 2 minutes. Don't cook the pork through as it will finish off cooking in the oven.

5   Add half of this mixture to the ricotta mixture. Mix well.

6   Lightly grease a flat baking dish, or line it with a damp baking paper.

7   Flatten the bread dough with your hands on a lightly floured table top. Place it on the baking dish, making sure to raise the edges so that the filling doesn't run over the side.

8   Fill the dough with the ricotta and pork mixture. Put the remaining beans, pork and onion mixture on top.

9   Sprinkle some sesame seeds if desired. Bake in the preheated oven for about 45 minutes.

 When fresh broad beans are not in season, you can either use the frozen ones or peas.

FISH AND POTATOES FTIRA

FTIRA BIL-ĦUT U PATATA

400g bread dough (not pizza dough)

300g potatoes, peeled and sliced very finely

100g onions, peeled and finely sliced

4 garlic cloves, peeled and finely chopped

2 tomatoes, deseeded and chopped

1 tin tuna chunks in oil, well drained

1 tin anchovies, drained

black olives, destoned

fresh basil, mint and marjoram, finely chopped

olive oil

sesame seeds (optional)

seasoning

1   Preheat the oven 190°C, gas mark 5.

2   Lightly grease a flat baking dish, or line it with a damp baking paper.

3   Flatten the bread dough with your hands on a lightly floured table top. Place it on the baking dish, making sure to raise the edges so that the filling doesn't run over the side.

4   Fill the dough with tuna, anchovies, tomatoes, garlic, olives and half of the onions. Sprinkle some herbs on top.

5   Put a layer of overlapping potato slices and the remaining onions and herbs on top. Pour some olive oil. Season and sprinkle with sesame seeds.

6   Bake in the oven for about 50 minutes until golden.

 For this *ftira*, the dough shouldn't be thick. In some villages, it is covered with another layer of dough. Instead of tinned tuna, you can use steak fish cut into very small pieces. You can also use very small fish like whitebait.

SMALL RICOTTA PIES

QASSATAT TAL-IRKOTTA

500g shortcrust pastry

200g ricotta

1 beaten egg

a separate beaten egg for glazing

finely chopped fresh parsley

freshly grated nutmeg

seasoning

1   Prepare the pastry.

2   Preheat the oven 190°C, gas mark 5.

3   Place the ricotta in a bowl and mash it well with a fork. Add the beaten egg, parsley, nutmeg and seasoning. Mix all the ingredients well together.

4   Roll out the pastry thinly. Cut smallish rounds out of the pastry and place a spoonful of filling on each round. Wrap the pastry up and around the filling, leaving a small gap at the top. Brush with beaten egg.

5   Place the qassatat either on a greased baking tray or on a tray lined with wet baking paper.

6   Bake for about 40 minutes. These small pies are best eaten warm.

 You can add a fresh local cheeselet to the ricotta. First, you will need to drain it completely. When fresh broad beans are in season, you can omit the parsley and add some to the ricotta. Remember to remove both skins beforehand.

SMALL PEA PIES

QASSATAT TAL-PIŻELLI

600g shortcrust pastry

400g dried peas

150g onions, peeled and chopped

a beaten egg for glazing

oil

seasoning

1   Prepare the pastry.

2   Soak the peas in plenty of water for at least 24 hours. You can add some bicarbonate of soda to the water to help soften them. Change the water at least every 3-4 hours.

3   Pour off all the water from the beans when they are done soaking. Don't use this water to cook the beans.

4   Place the beans in a strainer and rinse them with cool water before cooking.

5   Boil in plenty of water. Drain well.

6   Preheat the oven 190°C, gas mark 5.

7   Heat some oil in a pan and lightly fry the onions. Add the peas and continue cooking for a couple of minutes. Check for seasoning.

8   Continue from instruction number 4 as for the 'Small Ricotta Pies' (see page 178).

FRIED TOMATOES AND ONIONS WITH EGGS

BALBULJATA

6 or 8 large ripe tomatoes

8 eggs

2 finely chopped onions

1 tbsp olive oil

25-50g butter

chopped garlic to taste (optional)

fresh basil

salt and pepper

1   Peel, deseed and chop the tomatoes. Put them in a bowl.

2   Heat some oil and butter in a medium sized pan. Fry the onions until soft. Add the garlic, tomatoes and seasoning. Cook on medium heat for about 10 minutes.

3   Beat the eggs lightly in a large mixing bowl and pour them over the tomatoes and onions. Lower the heat and add the remaining butter and basil.

4   Stir continuously, as you would with scrambled eggs, over low heat until the eggs are barely set.

5   Serve immediately with fresh, Maltese, crusty bread, toast or *ftira*.

SWEETS

SPONGE FLAN FILLED WITH RICOTTA

FLAN TAL-PANEDISPANJA MIMLIJA BL-IRKOTTA

1 sponge flan, 22cm in diameter

800g ricotta

300g sugar

300g mixed, chopped, candied peel and chocolate chips

lightly toasted almonds and hazelnuts, chopped in medium sized pieces

1 freshly grated lemon rind

any liqueur of your choice

freshly grated nutmeg

red and green candied cherries for decoration

1   Prepare a sponge flan.

2   Put the ricotta and sugar in a large mixing bowl and mash well until you obtain a creamy mixture. If the ricotta is rather dry, add some milk or cream. Take about 2 or 3 tablespoons of ricotta and put them aside for decoration.

3   Add the candied peel and chocolate chips to the ricotta and mix well. Add the lemon rind and grated nutmeg. Mix well.

4   Put the flan on a large serving dish. Choose one that is as flat as possible.

5   Moisten the flan's surface with your chosen liqueur. Fill it with the ricotta mixture.

6   Spread the extra ricotta on the flan's edges and sprinkle the toasted nuts on it.

7   Decorate with the red and green candied cherries. Cool it in the fridge before serving.

 If you will be serving this flan to children, substitute the liqueur with fruit juice.

SWEET RICOTTA AND ALMOND TART

TORTA TAL-IRKOTTA ĦELWA U LEWŻ

600g sweet shortcrust pastry
600g ricotta
300ml fresh cream
200g pure ground almonds
120g sugar
100g candied peel
75g almonds, chopped in large pieces
60g candied cherries, cut in quarters
40g flaked almonds
3 whole eggs
1 egg, lightly beaten
grated rind of 1 lemon and 1 orange

1   Prepare the pastry. While the pastry is resting, start the filling.

2   Put the ricotta in a large mixing bowl together with the fresh cream. Beat together until the two ingredients are thoroughly combined and the mixture is of a creamy texture.

3   Add the sugar, ground almonds, chopped almonds as well as the lemon and orange rinds. Continue beating. Add the candied peel and chopped cherries. Mix well with a wooden spoon. Add the eggs and continue beating. The mixture should have a dropping consistency.

4   Preheat the oven 180°C, gas mark 4.

5   Roll out the pastry thinly on a lightly floured surface and line a 24cm diameter non-stick baking dish with it. Use a loose bottomed tin if available. This will make it easier to remove the cooked tart.

6   Press it lightly and firmly all over the base and sides of the tin, easing any overlapping pastry back down the sides as it is important not to stretch this bit too much.

7   Trim the edges. Prick the base all over with a fork and spoon the filling into the pastry case. Moisten the pastry's edges with a little water. Cut the remaining pastry in strips and form a grid with them.

8   Brush the pastry strips with beaten egg and decorate with the flaked almonds.

9   Bake for around 50-60 minutes in the preheated oven, until the pastry turns to a golden colour.

SINIZZA

800g sweet shortcrust pastry
cooked sponge cake
400g ricotta
80g sugar
60g candied cherries
1 beaten egg
grated lemon rind
apricot jam
white liqueur
vanilla essence

1   Grease a loaf tin or line it with baking paper. If you will be using baking paper, wet it slightly before lining the tin. Roll out the pastry quite thinly on a lightly floured surface and line the loaf tin with it. Leave some pastry for the top.

2   Cut thin slices of sponge cake and spread some apricot jam on them.

3   Use these slices to cover the bottom and sides of the pastry, jam side facing the pastry.

4   Put the ricotta in a mixing bowl. Add the sugar and liqueur. Mix well until you obtain a creamy texture.

5   Quarter the cherries and add them together with the vanilla essence and the grated lemon rind to the ricotta mixture. Mix well.

6   Cut some more slices of sponge cake.

7   Preheat the oven 180°C, gas mark 4.

8   Fill the loaf tin with the ricotta mixture. Smooth the top and cover it with the sponge cake slices. Spread some more jam on them.

9   Moisten the edges of the pastry with a little water. Cover with the remaining pastry. Seal well and trim the edges.

10   Make some slits in the top, brush with beaten egg and bake for around 60 minutes in the preheated oven.

11   Leave the sinizza to cool completely before removing it from the tin and slicing it.

MALTESE TRIFLE

TRIFLE STIL MALTI

cooked sponge cake
300g ricotta
300ml fresh cream
100g sugar
1 pkt strawberry jelly
any liqueur of your choice
candied cherries
walnuts or roasted almonds

For the custard

600ml milk
120g sugar
40g custard powder

1   Begin by preparing the custard. Put ¾ of the milk and sugar in a casserole. Put the mixture on moderate heat until it starts to boil.

2   Dilute the custard powder in the remaining milk and add it to the boiled milk. Cook for few minutes, stirring all the time. Remove it from over the heat and leave it to cool.

3   Slice the sponge thickly and cover the bottom of a large serving dish with the cut slices.

4   Prepare the strawberry jelly following the instructions on the packet, but using only two-thirds of the amount of water indicated. Pour the jelly mixture over the sponges and let them soak.

5   Either add the custard immediately or leave it until the sponges are well soaked with jelly. Put the trifle aside until the custard settles.

6   Cream together the fresh cream and the ricotta in a mixing bowl. Add the sugar and your chosen liqueur. Mix well.

7   Spread the ricotta mixture over the custard.

8   Decorate with cherries and walnuts or roasted almonds.

PASTRY HORNS FILLED WITH RICOTTA

KANNOLI TAL-IRKOTTA

For these *kannoli* you need metal tubes. These can be bought from those shops that sell cooking aids.

For the pastry
175g plain flour
25g margarine
red wine
water

For the filling
400g ricotta
100g candied cherries
100g roasted almonds
75g chocolate chips
75g icing sugar
frying oil

1   Sift the flour in a large mixing bowl and rub in the margarine until the mixture resembles breadcrumbs.

2   Add the red wine and enough water to make a dough. Knead until the dough is smooth. Cover it with stretch and seal and leave it to rest.

3   Prepare the filling while the pastry is resting.

4   Put the ricotta in a bowl and mash it well. Add the chocolate chips, cherries and chopped, roasted almonds. Mix well. Add the sugar and continue mixing.

5   Roll the pastry out thinly. Cut it into rounds with a cutter and wrap each round over a tube.

6   Heat some oil in a large saucepan.

7   Deep fry the *kannoli* tubes in boiling oil until golden brown. Pay special attention when frying them since boiling oil can be very dangerous.

8   Put the cooked *kannoli* on kitchen paper until all the oil is absorbed.

9   Once cooled, fill them with the ricotta mixture. The *kannoli* should always be filled at the last possible moment so that the cooked dough remains crunchy.

10   If you will be serving these *kannoli* for a special occasion, decorate each end with half of a candied cherry and dust them with icing sugar.

MARMURAT TART

TORTA TAL-MARMURAT

600g sweet shortcrust pastry

150g cake crumbs or digestive biscuits

150g ground almonds

120g candied peel

100g sugar

100g blanched almonds

80g chocolate chips

25g cocoa powder

2 eggs

2 tbsp jam

vanilla essence

For decoration

melted chocolate

royal icing

almond or sugar paste

candied cherries

1   Put the almonds in a heavy bottomed, ungreased frying pan. Stir often over medium heat until golden brown.

2   You can also roast the almonds in the oven. Preheat the oven to 180°C, gas mark 4. Spread the almonds in one layer on an ungreased, shallow baking dish. Bake for 10 to 15 minutes, stirring occasionally, until golden.

3   Leave the almonds to cool completely before chopping them in medium sized pieces.

4   Preheat the oven 190°C, gas mark 5.

5   Put all the dry filling ingredients into a bowl and stir them together.

6   Roll out the pastry thinly on a lightly floured surface and line a 24cm diameter non-stick baking dish with it. Use a loose bottomed tin if available. This will make it easier to remove the cooked tart.

7   Press it lightly and firmly all over the base and sides of the tin, easing any overlapping pastry back down the sides as it is important not to stretch this bit too much.

8   Trim the edges, but leaving a small edge of pastry sticking over the edge of the flan dish to allow for shrinkage in the oven.

9   Prick the base all over with a fork and spread some jam over the pastry.

10   Spoon the filling into the pastry case and flatten it with a palette knife or the back of a spoon.

11   Bake in the preheated oven for about 45 minutes.

12   Leave the tart to cool completely before removing it from the tin.

13   Decorate with melted chocolate, almond or sugar paste, royal icing and candied cherries.

BREAD PUDDING

PUDINA TAL-ĦOBŻ

The Maltese bread pudding is very different from the English bread and butter pudding. It is done with leftover, stale bread. There is no standard recipe for this dish; the exact ingredients vary from family to family and whatever dried fruit you find in the cupboard!

A piece of warm *pudina tal-ħobż* served with a hot cup of coffee or tea is something that everyone should savour!

500g stale bread
600ml milk
200g sugar
100g margarine
100g sultanas
100g currants
40g drinking chocolate powder
40g cocoa powder
3 eggs
grated rind of ½ lemon
grated rind of ½ orange
mixed spice
cinnamon
freshly grated nutmeg
vanilla essence

1   Place the bread in a large mixing bowl. Cover it completely with water and let it soak for 15 minutes. Put the bread in a colander and allow it to drain properly. Use your hands to remove as much water as possible.

2   Preheat the oven 180°C, gas mark 4.

3   Grease and flour a large baking dish.

4   Cut the margarine in small pieces and add them to the bread. Mix well.

5   Add all the other ingredients. Continue mixing until all the ingredients blend completely.

6   Pour the mixture into the baking dish.

7   Level its top with the back of a spoon.

8   Bake for 40-50 minutes.

9   This pudding can be served either warm or cold.

PRINJOLATA

The hundreds of *prinjolati* filling the confectioneries all over the Maltese Islands are a sure sign that Carnival is approaching! The *prinjolata* is a delicious sweet made of sweet shortcrust pastry biscuits, candied fruit, cream, nuts and chocolate, all covered with Italian meringue. Its name derives from the word *prinjoli*, the Maltese name for pine nuts. Once ready, it resembles a snow capped mountain!

1. SWEET SHORTCRUST BISCUITS

GALLETTINI TAL-GĦAĠINA ĦELWA

600g sweet shortcrust pastry

1 Preheat the oven 180°C, gas mark 4.

2 Put the dough on a lightly floured surface and knead it lightly. Form the dough into a long, round shape and cut it into walnut sized pieces. Flatten and shape each piece into a small biscuit.

3 Put the biscuits on a greased baking tray.

4 Bake for 15-20 minutes or until pale golden in colour.

2. CONFECTIONER'S CUSTARD

KREMA PASTIĊĊIERA

Nowadays, in supermarkets and large grocery shops, you can find this custard in powdered form. All you have to do is to add it either to milk or water. It is quite easy to make and you can be sure that the end result will be perfect. Should you wish to prepare this type of custard, cook it according to the directions on the packet and then continue from instruction number 5 of the recipe given below.

On the other hand, if you prefer to have homemade custard, this is the recipe to follow.

600ml milk
400ml fresh cream
100g sugar
40g cornflour
2 egg yolks
vanilla essence

1 Put the egg yolks and about one-third of the sugar in a bowl. Whisk until they are pale and leave a slight trail when you lift up the whisk. Sift in the cornflour and mix well.

2 Place the milk, the remaining sugar and the vanilla essence in a saucepan and bring the mixture just to boiling point.

3 Lower the heat. Gradually, add the hot milk to the egg yolk mixture. Cook over low heat, stirring constantly, for 3 to

4 minutes until the mixture thickens. Remove it from over the heat.

4   Pour the custard into a bowl and let it cool, stirring occasionally to prevent a skin from forming. Ideally, the custard should be spread on a marble slab. That way it will cool in a shorter time. You have to stir it to prevent a skin from forming just the same.

5   When you are absolutely sure that the custard is completely cold, place it in a mixer and beat it well.

6   Add the fresh cream and continue beating until you have a creamy consistency.

3. ITALIAN MERINGUE

XKUMA STIL TALJAN

Italian meringue is the only meringue suitable for coating the *prinjolata*. This is because its soft but pliable consistency can be spooned over and peaked loosely with a spoon. Other meringues deflate quickly.

Since Italian meringue is made with the addition of a boiling sugar syrup, using a sugar thermometer is of great help.

300g sugar
150g egg whites
90g water
1 tsp of cream of tartar

1   Combine the sugar and water in a small pan and bring the mixture to a boil, stirring continuously with a wooden spoon until the sugar dissolves. The temperature should be 116°C.

2   Start whisking the egg whites with the cream of tartar in a clean, grease-free bowl of an electric mixer until soft peaks form.

3   Meanwhile, bring the sugar syrup to 121°C (hard ball stage). Increase speed to high and, with motor running, gradually pour the syrup into the meringue.

4   Beat at medium speed until the meringue cools to room temperature and is thick and glossy (15-20 minutes).

4. FINISH THE PRINJOLATA

KIF TIBNI L-PRINJOLATA

sweet shortcrust biscuits
confectioner's custard
Italian meringue
80g roasted almonds
80g walnuts
60g roasted pine nuts
20g pine nuts
20g pistachio nuts
red candied cherries
dark chocolate
any liqueur of your choice

1 Put aside some cherries, almonds, walnuts and pine nuts for decoration.

2 Place the biscuits in a large mixing bowl. Pour your chosen liqueur over them.

3 Add the confectioner's custard, walnuts, almonds, roasted pine nuts and cherries. Mix well.

4 Line 1 medium sized bowl or 2 small ones with stretch and seal.

5 Fill the bowl with the *prinjolata* mixture. Cover well with stretch and seal. Firmly press the mixture down and put the bowl in the fridge for at least a couple of hours.

6 Remove the *prinjolata* from the bowl and place it on a flat plate. Remove the stretch and seal film gently.

7 Melt the chocolate according to the *bain marie* technique.

8 Cover the *prinjolata* with Italian meringue and decorate with the melted chocolate, cherries, various nuts and pistachios.

LENTEN ALMOND SWEET

KWAREŻIMAL

Kwareżimal is a traditional Maltese sweet made during Lent. The word *kwareżimal* refers to *quaresima*, literally the *quadragesima*, the forty days of Lent. It contains no fat. Long ago, it used to be made without eggs since these were not eaten during Lent. Nowadays, since the Lenten fast is no longer adhered to, egg whites are added to the ingredients to make them tastier.

250g almonds
250g sugar
240g plain flour
2 egg whites
Maltese honey
grated rind of 1 orange
ground cloves
orange flower water
water

1   Lightly toast or roast the almonds.

2   Leave the almonds to cool completely and grind them coarsely. Leave some for sprinkling on top of the *kwareżimal*.

3   Sift the flour in a large mixing bowl. Add the almonds, sugar, grated orange rind, orange flower water, ground cloves and egg whites.

4   Knead lightly until all the ingredients are well mixed. If the dough is too stiff, add some water. Be careful when adding water since the dough shouldn't be soft. Otherwise, it will flatten during baking.

5   Preheat the oven 190°C, gas mark 5.

6   Lightly wet your hands and start forming the dough into ovals. Each piece should be approximately 16cm long, 5cm wide and about 2cm thick.

7   Lightly grease a baking tray or line it with baking paper.

8   Place the *kwareżimal* pieces on the baking tray.

9   Prior to baking make a criss-cross pattern on the *kwareżimal* with the tip of a sharp knife.

10   Bake for about 20-25 minutes.

11   The *kwareżimal* should still be soft once you remove them from the oven. They will harden upon cooling. Therefore, don't make the mistake of leaving them in the oven until they harden. If you do so, be certain that by the time they will have cooled, they will be as hard as marble and no one will eat them!

12   While still hot, spread the *kwareżimal* with Maltese honey and press on the chopped, roasted almonds.

FIGOLLA

The *figolla* is a sweet made of shortcrust pastry with an almond filling. It is given as a gift on Easter Sunday. Prepared in a variety of shapes, it is decorated either with royal icing or with chocolate.

800g sweet shortcrust pastry (see page 36)

For the filling

300g pure ground almonds

220g sugar

4 egg whites

grated rind of 1 lemon

vanilla essence

1   To make 4 *figolli* you have to use 1,440g flour. This means that you have to make the basic pastry recipe and multiply all the ingredients by 3.

2   Prepare the filling while the pastry is resting.

3   Put the ground almonds, sugar, eggs, grated rind of 1 lemon, essence and egg whites in a large mixing bowl. Mix well together until you have a fairly dry paste.

4   Preheat the oven 190°C, gas mark 5.

5   Place the pastry on a lightly floured board. Cut a piece the size of 1 *figolla* and roll it out. You shouldn't roll out the pastry too thinly or it will easily break.

6   Choose the shape of the *figolla* and cut 2 pieces of the same shape. Put 1 shape on a greased baking tin which you can otherwise line with baking paper.

7   Brush the sides with water or beaten egg. Spread with the almond paste. Leave a free space all around for sealing. Put the other piece of pastry very carefully on top. Seal all around by pressing with your fingers.

8   Bake for 30 minutes or until the pastry is golden brown.

9   Leave the *figolla* to cool in the baking tray. Once cooled, remove it from the tray and put it on a wire tray until it becomes completely cold.

10   If your oven is large enough, you can bake more than 1 *figolla* at a time.

11   Finally, you can decorate each *figolla* with royal icing, little silver balls and a small chocolate egg pressed in the centre.

BONE-SHAPED FILLED BISCUITS

GĦADAM

The Maltese calendar year is packed with feasts both secular and religious, and generally specific traditional food items are linked with them. One of these is All Souls' Day, the Christian day of the dead, which is celebrated on the 2nd of November.

Confectioners' shops are filled with sweets shaped like bones. They are made using the same recipe as for the *figolli*, but the dough is shaped so as to resemble a bone. This is then covered with white icing to render it even more similar to a bone. These sweets can be found throughout the whole month of November.

800g sweet shortcrust pastry

300g pure ground almonds

300g sugar

egg whites

grated rind of 1 lemon

vanilla essence

1   Put the ground almonds, sugar, eggs, grated rind of 1 lemon, essence and egg whites in a large mixing bowl. Don't add too much almond essence as it will give the filling a bitter taste. Mix the ingredients well together until you have a fairly dry paste.

2   Preheat the oven 190°C, gas mark 5.

3   Place the pastry on a lightly floured table top and roll it out. Cut it into oblongs.

4   Put some almond paste in the centre of each oblong. Wrap the pastry around the filling and mould them into the traditional bone shape. Tuck the pastry neatly around, trimming off extra bits.

5   Put these 'bones' on a baking tray that has been lined with baking paper.

6   Bake for about 30 minutes or until they are golden brown.

7   Remove them from the tray and leave them to cool.

8   When completely cold, cover the 'bones' with white royal icing.

HOT COCOA DRINK WITH CHESTNUTS

IMBULJUTA TAL-QASTAN

Imbuljuta is the traditional Maltese drink served after Midnight Mass on Christmas and New Year's Eve. It is the perfect recipe for those special nights where you want something hot, spicy and deliciously seasonal. This drink has that wonderful Christmassy smell to it, with cloves, cinnamon, chocolate as well as orange and tangerine rinds as ingredients. Generally, it is served piping hot in mugs or small bowls.

400g dried chestnuts
175g sugar
50g drinking chocolate
50g dark chocolate, chopped in large pieces
1 tangerine peel, finely chopped
1 orange rind, grated
ground cloves
mixed spice

1   Wash the chestnuts a couple of times, changing the water after every wash. Place the chestnuts in a large bowl, cover them with water again and allow to soak overnight.

2   The next day, first take off any remaining peel, then put all the chestnuts and the water into a large saucepan. Add all the other ingredients.

3   Put on moderate heat until the mix starts boiling.

4   Reduce the heat and simmer for about 50 minutes or until the chestnuts are tender. Add some boiling water if necessary.

SWEET PASTRY RINGS WITH TREACLE

QAGĦAQ TAL-GĦASEL

Qagħaq tal-għasel are sweet pastry rings filled with a treacle mixture. Literally translated they are 'honey rings', but there is absolutely no honey in the recipe. The main ingredient in the filling is treacle. In Maltese treacle is known as *għasel iswed*; most probably that is why they are known as honey rings. Years ago village people used q*astanija*, and not treacle, for their *qagħaq tal-għasel*. This was made by melting down honey-combs after the honey had been extracted from them. In all probability q*astanija* is a corruption of the Italian *castagna*, which means chestnut. It might be that it was so called because the mixture was the colour of chestnuts. But there are absolutely no chestnuts in the mixture. Through the years q*astanija* was substituted by black treacle. For those who have a very sweet tooth, sugar is added to the filling mixture.

For the pastry

500g plain flour

50g margarine

3 egg yolks

water or anisette liqueur

For the filling

400ml water

400g black treacle or golden syrup or a combination of both

180g semolina

100g sugar

3 tbsp orange flower water

2 tbsp cocoa powder

1 tbsp mixed spice

1 tbsp aniseeds

grated rind of a tangerine, lemon and orange

1 Prepare the pastry by following exactly the same method for sweet shortcrust pastry.

2 Prepare the filling while the pastry is resting.

3 Place all the ingredients, except for the semolina, in a large saucepan and slowly bring the mix to a boil. You have to stir all the time.

4 Add the semolina very slowly to the boiling mixture, stirring all the time.

5 Bring again to a boil. Cook for a further 5 minutes. It is very important that you stir all the time; otherwise the semolina will stick to the saucepan's bottom.

6 Remove the mixture from over the heat and place it in a large bowl. Once cooled, cover the bowl with stretch and seal and leave overnight in the fridge.

7 The next day, cut the pastry into 8 pieces. Roll out each piece and give it a rectangular shape.

8 Preheat the oven 180°C, gas mark 4.

9 Lightly dust a table top with semolina. Take spoonfuls of the filling and curve them into S shapes. The shapes have to fit the rectangles.

10 If the filling is rather sticky, just add more semolina on the table top.

11 Place one of the S shapes on each rectangle of pastry. Roll it like a small Swiss roll. Place it cut side down and lightly moisten the ends with water. Bring the ends together to form a ring. Pinch ends together to seal. Make a series of decorative slashes on the top with a sharp knife.

12 Place the pastry rings on a baking tray that has previously been well dusted with semolina.

13 Bake for about 15-20 minutes or until the pastry obtains a very light beige colour. In the case of these pastry rings, the pastry should never turn golden brown.

DATE FILLED PASTRIES

IMQARET

Imqaret is the plural of *maqrut*. The word *maqrut* derives from an Arabic word meaning 'a diamond shape'.

In fact, *imqaret* are delicious, mouth-watering, diamond shaped pastries stuffed with dates and deep fried. They are certainly not for the figure conscious! If you want to reduce the amount of calories, you can always bake them instead; the taste though is not the same as that of those deep fried.

Imqaret are best eaten hot; the baked ones are just as good at room temperature.

For the pastry
650g plain flour
175g margarine
85g sugar
1 beaten egg
1 tsp baking powder

For the filling
360g dates, pitted and chopped
grated rind of 1 orange
orange flower water
aniseed liqueur

1 Sift the flour together with the baking powder. Rub the margarine into the flour until the mixture resembles breadcrumbs. Add the sugar and mix well.

2 Bind with the beaten egg to make a dough. Leave the pastry to rest for 30 minutes.

3 Prepare the filling while the pastry is resting.

4 Place all the ingredients for the filling into a saucepan and cook over low heat, stirring occasionally. Allow to simmer until the whole mixture becomes creamy.

5 Remove from the heat. Put the mixture in a bowl and leave it to cool.

6 Put the pastry on a lightly floured surface. Roll it out into a 10cm wide strip.

7 Moisten the pastry's edges, place the date mixture down the middle of the long strip of pastry and fold over to enclose the date filling. Press the edges tightly together.

8 Cut diagonally across the pastry into 5cm long diamond shaped *imqaret* with a sharp knife.

9 Deep fry them in boiling oil until golden brown. Boiling oil can be very dangerous; pay special attention when handling *imqaret* at this stage.

10 Drain thoroughly and serve hot.

PASTRY RINGS

QAGĦAQ ĦELWIN

These rings are a local delicacy and you might still find a small village bakery here and there where they are made. Otherwise, you have to buy them from supermarkets and small grocery shops. They can be eaten either straight from the packet or else dipped in hot milk, tea or coffee.

300g plain flour

150g sugar

100g margarine

12g baking ammonia

2 small eggs

1 tsp baking powder

grated rind of ½ orange and ½ lemon

juice of ½ orange and ½ lemon

vanilla essence

sesame seeds

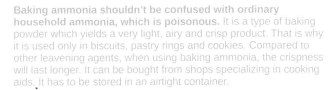

Baking ammonia shouldn't be confused with ordinary household ammonia, which is poisonous. It is a type of baking powder which yields a very light, airy and crisp product. That is why it is used only in biscuits, pastry rings and cookies. Compared to other leavening agents, when using baking ammonia, the crispness will last longer. It can be bought from shops specializing in cooking aids. It has to be stored in an airtight container.

1 Sieve the flour and baking ammonia into a large bowl, holding the sieve as high as possible so that the flour gets a really good airing.

2 Cut the margarine into smallish lumps. Add it to the flour mixture and rub it in using only your fingertips and being as light as possible. As you gently rub the fat into the flour, lift it up high and let it fall back into the bowl, which again means that all the time air is being incorporated. Do this just long enough to make the mixture crumbly with a few odd lumps here and there.

3 Add the orange and lemon zests and the juice. Mix well.

4 Add the eggs and vanilla essence and work into a smooth and elastic dough. Put it in a plastic bag or wrap it in stretch and seal. Leave it to rest for at least half an hour. You can prepare the dough the day before and leave it in the fridge overnight.

5 Put the dough on a lightly floured surface and knead it lightly. Divide it in small pieces around 60g each.

6 Preheat the oven 190°C, gas mark 5.

7 Work each dough into a small ball. Roll it between your hands to form a long shape. You can then give it round-ended finger shaped ends, or else twist the pastry into circles and press the ends together. You can also shape it into the figure eight.

8 You can either leave these pastry rings plain or else sprinkled with sesame seeds. In the latter case, place some sesame seeds on a flat plate and press the pastry shapes into the seeds.

9 Arrange the pastry shapes on a well greased baking tray or one lined with baking paper. Bake for about 20-25 minutes or until they turn golden in colour.

ORANGE CAKE

KEJK TAL-LARINĠ

Sunny Malta is famous for its oranges, especially the blood red ones. The Maltese village of Lija is famous for its oranges since practically every household has its own orange grove. A yearly Orange Festival is organised by the Lija Local Council, where one can find all types of products made with oranges.

250g flour '00'
225g eggs
180g sugar
120g margarine
60g butter
1 tbsp oil
½ tsp baking powder
½ tsp glycerine
juice of ½ orange
grated zest of an orange
vanilla essence
margarine and flour for greasing the cake tin

1   Preheat the oven to 180°C, gas mark 4. You will need a 28cm cake tin well greased with margarine and dusted with flour.

2   Sieve the flour and baking powder in a bowl.

3   Cream the butter and sugar well until light and fluffy. Use a food processor or an electric hand whisk.

4   Add the eggs one by one, beating well after each addition. Add the zest, vanilla essence, oil and glycerine. Leave some zest for decorating.

5   Fold in the sieved flour. Slowly add the orange juice until it is incorporated.

6   Now the mixture should just have a dropping consistency. Add some more orange juice if necessary.

7   Pour the batter into the prepared cake tin. Bake for 1 hour and 15 minutes or until an inserted skewer comes out clean.

8   Before removing the cake from the tin, leave it within the tin on a wire rack to cool.

9   Decorate with the remaining orange zest.

LEMON GRANITA

GRANITA TAL-LUMI

Granita is a semi-frozen dessert made from water, sugar and various flavourings. It originated in Sicily, where it is still very popular. Some time ago, I was in Sicily attending a congress organised by the Federation of Italian Cooks. I was told that, according to legend, the first *granita* was made with ice brought from Mount Etna.

600ml water
800g sugar
5 lemons
1 glass white wine
3 egg whites

1   Put the water, sugar and wine in a large pan.

2   Put on moderate heat and cook. Boil until the mixture becomes a thick, but clear syrup.

3   Remove from the heat and leave to cool for 15 minutes. Strain into a bowl.

4   Squeeze the lemons, taking care to discard the pips.

5   Add the lemon juice to the syrup. Mix and let the mixture cool completely.

6   Add the egg whites when the mixture has completely cooled. The egg whites shouldn't be beaten. Mix well.

7   Pour the mixture into a freezing dish, cover it and place it in the freezer.

CONVERSION TABLES

All these are approximate conversions.

Never mix metric and imperial measures in one recipe; stick to one system or the other. All spoon measurements are level, unless specified otherwise.

[1] A pint isn't always a pint: in British, Australian and often Canadian recipes you will see an imperial pint listed as 20 fluid ounces. American and some Canadian recipes use the American pint measurement, which is 16 fluid ounces.

[1] Liquid Conversions

Imperial	Metric	American
½ fl oz	15 ml	1 tbsp
1 fl oz	30 ml	1/8 cup
2 fl oz	60 ml	¼ cup
4 fl oz	120 ml	½ cup
8 fl oz	240 ml	1 cup
16 fl oz	480 ml	1 pint

Weights

Imperial	Metric
½ oz	10 g
¾ oz	20 g
1 oz	25 g
1½ oz	40 g
2 oz	50 g
2½ oz	60 g
3 oz	75 g
4 oz	110 g
4½ oz	125 g
5 oz	150 g
6 oz	175 g
7 oz	200 g
8 oz	225 g
9 oz	250 g
10 oz	275 g
12 oz	350 g
1 lb	450 g
1 lb 8 oz	700 g
2 lb	900 g
3 lb	1.35 kg

Volume

Imperial	Metric
2 fl oz	55 ml
3 fl oz	75 ml
5 fl oz (¼ pint)	150 ml
10 fl oz (½ pint)	275 ml
1 pints	570 ml
1¼ pints	725 ml
1¾ pints	1 litre
2 pints	1.2 litres
2½ pints	1.5 litres
4 pints	2.25 litres

[2] Oven Temperatures

Gas Mark	°F	°C
1	275°F	140°C
2	300°F	150°C
3	325°F	170°C
4	350°F	180°C
5	375°F	190°C
6	400°F	200°C
7	425°F	220°C
8	450°F	230°C
9	475°F	240°C

American Cup Conversions

American	Imperial	Metric
1 cup flour	5 oz	150 g
1 cup caster/ granulated sugar	8 oz	225 g
1 cup brown sugar	6 oz	175 g
1 cup butter/ margarine/ lard	8 oz	225 g
1 cup sultanas/ raisins	7 oz	200 g
1 cup currants	5 oz	150 g
1 cup ground almonds	4 oz	110 g
1 cup golden syrup	12 oz	350 g
1 cup uncooked rice	7 oz	200 g
1 cup grated cheese	4 oz	110 g

[2] If using a fan oven you will need to reduce the oven temperature in a recipe by 15 degrees.

INDEX